Career Coaching Your ADHD Teen

How to take charge of the 9 Key Issues stopping your teen make a successful career choice

By
Jenny Booth

Illustrated by Steve Lee

MAPLE
PUBLISHERS

Career Coaching Your ADHD Teen

Author: Jenny Booth

Copyright © 2025 Jenny Booth

The right of Jenny Booth to be identified as author of this work has been asserted by the author in accordance with section 77 and 78 of the Copyright, Designs and Patents Act 1988.

First Published in 2025

ISBN 978-1-83538-617-0 (Paperback)
978-1-83538-618-7 (E-Book)

Book Cover Design and Book Layout by:
White Magic Studios
www.whitemagicstudios.co.uk

Published by:
Maple Publishers
Fairbourne Drive, Atterbury,
Milton Keynes,
MK10 9RG, UK
www.maplepublishers.com

Disclaimer

A CIP catalogue record for this title is available from the British Library.

All rights reserved. No part of this book may be reproduced or translated in any form or by any means, electronic or mechanical, including photocopying, recording or by any information storage and retrieval system without written permission from the author.

This book reflects the author's personal recollections of experiences over time. Some names and characteristics have been changed, some events have been condensed, and certain dialogues have been recreated. While every effort has been made to ensure accuracy, the author has also drawn upon publicly available sources and online research. The Publisher and the author disclaim any responsibility for errors, omissions, or any outcomes resulting from the use of this material.

For Joe. My reason for everything.

Contents

Disclaimer 3

Acknowledgments 9

Introduction 13

Chapter 1 – ADHD & Executive Functioning 19

Chapter 2 – Where Do I Start? 27

Chapter 3 – Key Issue Number 1 Procrastination 35

Chapter 4 – Key Issue Number 2 Boredom 49

Chapter 5 – Key Issue Number 3 Self Esteem & Self Belief ... 61

Chapter 6 – Key Issue Number 4 Rejection Sensitivity
    Dysphoria (RSD) 73

Chapter 7 – Key Issue Number 5 Masking 83

Chapter 8 – Key Issue Number 6 Social Anxiety 93

Chapter 9 – Key Issue Number 7 The Sensory Stuff 103

Chapter 10 – Key Issue Number 8 ADHD Freeze (a.k.a. Overwhelm) . 115

Chapter 11 – Key Issue Number 9 Time Blindness 125

1. Research Pilot Details 144
2. Careers Tool Kit 145
3. Useful Links 150
4. Additional Reading 151

Acknowledgments

This book wouldn't have been possible without the unwavering support and love from my husband Al. My rock. Gentle advice when I needed it with a tiny dose of constructive criticism. Keeping the home fires burning while I sat writing with my 'thinking cap' on.

My beautiful boy Joe who keeps me on my toes & helped me come up with my 9 key issues so eloquently.

My Mum whose unconditional love & pride pushes me forward every day.

Memories of my Dad's "I've got every confidence" in times of self-doubt...of which there are many.

Not forgetting good friends Sarah Sinclair, Jean Lippett, & Emma Bird who bought into my ADHD passion early doors and listened till their ears rang!

Steve Lee who has drawn the most wonderful illustrations at very short notice.

Heidi Woolley from University of St. Augustine, Florida for her insight into occupational therapy and ADHD. Also, thanks to the many colleagues and friends who helped me to explore the links between ADHD and youth unemployment.

You all made a difference.

Quotes from parents:

"She always struggled at school and got low grades which was so disheartening for her as she tried so hard. Luckily her personality outshone her academic skills and I always told her I was proud of her. We celebrated her low grades. She went to college but it was never for her. Her personality got her a job then she met & chatted to the right people…but then the hard work needed to kick in. Her ADHD must have been soul destroying for her as her hopes & dreams would be shattered if she didn't get through…I have never seen someone work so hard. I am so proud of her, how she battled through, against the odds. She is now held in high esteem by colleagues and management alike. Love my girl!"

"He was written off in school and not really moved forward. He still can't decide what he wants to do with his life and struggles to be motivated to go to work. He's super social but now I realise that he was masking a lot of other things."

"She was so quiet in school and never got in any trouble. I think she just struggled to listen and found it all a bit boring! She struggled to make a decision to do anything really. Thankfully she met someone whose job interested her and that seemed to motivate her to do well."

"He wasn't diagnosed in his grammar school and his academic achievement reduced significantly once he was 14. He was excluded ten weeks before his GCSEs started. His motivation, chronically low self- esteem & trauma from school left him unable to engage with job searching or keeping a job. He is now diagnosed ADHD and on an appropriate treatment plan. He is fully engaged in his career now but those lost years & ongoing trauma scars he will carry forever."

Introduction

Having spent over 30 years as a Careers Adviser supporting young people to plan their futures - my mindset changed. Lightbulb moment... Epiphany.... Call it what you will but something within me changed! I started to look at the barriers facing teenagers to progress in a different way. My observations are from personal and professional lived experience, and I hope that by sharing them I can help parents and professionals make sense of what can get in the way of career planning. This isn't a medical book.... I am nowhere near qualified for that! However, what I do have is masses of experience working with young people and heaps of empathy and understanding. Just loads of "I've got your back!"

I have spent hours & hours chatting to teenagers and young adults about their ideas and where they see their strengths and weaknesses. Many hours trying to guide them through their thoughts and feelings to come up with some kind of master plan that they can follow to become a 'successful human being'.

I have done this in careers centres, schools, colleges, community centres, libraries, cafes, their own homes and cupboards. Ok, so not really a cupboard but a tiny, dusty space that is left for this deemed 'non- important' discussion by managers restricted by resources. A tiny space which seems at odds with the size of the decision that these teens are expected to make. A space where they are expected to come up with the answer to that question... you know the one.... **"Do you know what you want to do?"**

Teenagers & THE Question!

The question asked by parents, teachers, aunties & uncles, grandparents the world over. The question that is asked of any awkward, gangly teenager so the adult can try to make sense of them and who they are.

"What's wrong with that?" The answer is that most teens are struggling to make sense of **themselves** and who **they** are which leaves them tongue tied. And now I'm going to throw a huge, unexploded bomb into the mix. A bomb that affects a proportion of our young people but is often hidden, unexplained or ignored. **That bomb is ADHD.**

I'm assuming that the reason that you have picked up this book is that you already have some understanding of ADHD. That you are a parent or a relative; a friend or a neighbour; a teacher or a key worker of a young person that is either already diagnosed with ADHD or is showing traits & symptoms. You may be the parent of one of our young people in the UK who is currently on an interminable waiting list for assessment for diagnosis of ADHD. Or you may be a professional that is desperate to discover more about helping these amazing teenagers sally forth into the big wide world.

For those who have picked up this book and are unsure about what ADHD actually is, I'll summarise the key symptoms and types shortly. However, this isn't a clinical ADHD book. Neither is it a specific 'how to parent your ADHD child' book.

Career Coaching & ADHD

I am going to enable you, as the reader, and someone who cares passionately about your young person, to coach and support them through a challenging decision. It's a tricky stage for any teenager but for our ADHDs it can become a nightmare. It can leave them disillusioned with the world and paralysed into inactivity. I will come on to the reasons for this later but for now, just assume that a decision that is tricky for all adolescents is a minefield for a young person with ADHD.

As it is so difficult, I believe that it cannot be done alone. It's just too big, too complicated, too messy! In some cases, it needs to be supported by a professional who understands ADHD and young people. This could be a Careers Adviser that you are confident really gets it; or it could be an ADHD Coach.

However, some of these careers services are just unavailable in the UK and it is unfortunately a postcode lottery. ADHD Coaches are only available at a cost at present which is just not affordable for many. Although teachers are often sympathetic and caring, their training in SEND (Special Educational Needs and Disabilities) is woeful and not ADHD specific. On top of this they are hugely busy people and just don't have the time to coach, guide and support one teen through this myriad of symptoms, ideas, and knowledge of career planning.

With knowledge about what the main issues are that impact ADHD young people planning their futures, I believe that you can be successful in guiding them through into living a fulfilling and successful life. It won't be easy! You will have many challenges and frustrations along the way. There will be times when you feel depleted and just in disbelief that you can help in anyway. But it is possible. You will get there. They need you by their side along this road. An adult who is willing to learn and understand. An adult who really cares about the issues they find difficult. An adult that doesn't measure their success and progress against another person's child who seems to do everything so easily!

You know the one…Head Girl? Captain of the football team? Has known what they want to do with their lives since the age of 5? Masses of work experience? Excelling at school or university? Has a job offer before finishing their studies? A huge list of extracurricular interests…. We don't call them neurotypical in our house… we call them neuro-tedious!

Yes, we all know one! Plus, a very 'proud' parent behind them who just adores to share how their child's life is swimming along just perfectly!

Don't be put off! It's ok! It will happen for your child too. It may be in a different way and at a different speed…but it will happen. They just need you as parent and negotiator along for the ride. I also believe that little Mr/Miss Perfect won't be as sure of themselves if you just look below the surface. So don't worry about them! Don't spend your precious time comparing and feeling disillusioned if your child manages school but not much else…or doesn't manage school at all.

There is a great deal of research out there that suggests a young person with ADHD is approximately 3 years behind their peers emotionally. Ponder on that for a minute…. now look at your teen with fresh eyes. They may be where they should be in terms of their physical development. They may have brilliant expressive language skills and cognitive ability that puts them ahead of their peers by miles. But as for their executive functioning and emotional maturity we are talking years behind. So, that six foot 16 year old will be operating at age 13 as far as decision making, and making rational, mature plans. Your sparky, articulate 13-year-old will be operating as a 10-year-old in many ways. Wow! With that in mind they are actually doing amazingly well. This mismatch of intelligence v emotional maturity has a huge impact on career planning. It is so easy to get drawn into very articulate arguments & debates as a parent only to realise sometime later that so much of it wasn't age appropriate for your teen. It just 'sounded' like it was. So frustrating!

However, imagine being that 16-year-old with a diagnosis of ADHD for a minute. Really try and put yourself in their shoes. Imagine a teacher going round the class of 30 pupils asking 'the big question' - "So, what is it you want to do as a career?" Imagine the answers: a nurse; an engineer; a vet; a plumber; etc, etc. With each convincing sounding job, the teacher gets closer and closer to your turn. Your heart begins to pound. Your palms begin to sweat. You have no idea what your plan is. Your mind flits from job to job and it all sounds childish! You know you can't say astronaut, footballer or princess but a big part of you wants to!!! So, what do you do? You come up with a job that sounds socially acceptable just for something to say. You have no idea what it really is and even if you would like it…but it stops the awkward silence or the interrogation into what is it you really want to do. Or you say 'Astronaut' as that is what you really want to do and then feel crushed by the eye rolls and sniggers that inevitably ricochet around the classroom.

Since my lightbulb moment, I have approached my parenting and my job in a different way. I have researched teenage ADHD and have realised that the sluggish executive functioning of the ADHD young person means that we must take on board nine key issues that affect rational decision making and planning. I will explore these issues one by one in the chapters to come, see how they present, and have a look at how we can help and overcome the obstacles that they bring.

Each chapter is designed to be dipped in to as a standalone or the issues can be read in their entirety! There is so much cross over between the issues described so you will see advice repeated. What works for one issue also works well for another! Simple!

I don't think I fully understood how disabling these issues are when trying to navigate the key decisions that other, 'neuro typical' young people seem to make so effortlessly. I hope that by writing this book I can pass on some of my observations and experiences that make life as a parent a little easier. A greater understanding of what is going on for your teen.

Chapter 1
ADHD & Executive Functioning

So, let's briefly have a look at what ADHD is.

ADHD stands for Attention Deficit Hyperactivity Disorder. A terrible title which includes not one but two negative terms. Deficit and Disorder! Hopefully this title will change soon as understanding and support improves, but for the moment, we are stuck with it.

There are 3 types of ADHD as follows:

Hyperactive & Impulsive ADHD:

This is the type of ADHD that most people will recognise. The stereotype of the constantly moving child. Full of energy and seemingly no fear. Noisy, chatty, and at times disruptive. Endless energy that no amount of activity tires out. Poor sleepers that can seemingly survive on just a couple of hours. Fuelled by adrenaline.

Inattentive ADHD:

This type of ADHD individual appears distracted, finds it hard to get motivated, procrastinates and is at higher risk of poor mental health. Often classed as the day dreamer. This used to be classed as ADD. My opinion is that the hyperactivity is still there, it is just internalised.

Combined ADHD:

Most young people diagnosed will be classed as 'Combined' meaning that they have enough traits and symptoms of both hyperactive and inattentive types.

I apologise if my descriptions are simplistic, but there is so much information out there that describes these types in more depth. Have a quick look online and you will come across some fabulous resources that further explain what ADHD is.

Check out your teen's diagnosis letter again or try and identify symptoms if not yet diagnosed. It will help as we get further into this book and explore the traits that can cause issues with career planning.

What is Executive Functioning?

So, we are told repeatedly that ADHD affects executive functioning. But what does this mean and how on earth does it have an impact on your child trying to plan for their future? Why doesn't my teen realise how important it is to have some kind of idea about the future?

Executive functioning is often called 'the management system of the brain'.

Wait a minute... the management system?! Let's break down what that involves. Let's define management as meaning:

- Goal setting
- Planning
- Getting things done.

If ADHD has a negative impact on executive functioning... it's no wonder your teen is struggling and possibly avoiding any thought of the big scary future. It's understandable. Wouldn't you?

Executive functioning can impact all areas of life. Working memory, flexibility of thought and self-control. So, what does this really mean for your young person? Whether they have a diagnosis of ADHD or are showing traits, they are likely to have difficulties with the following:

Listening carefully. Yes, that part that drives you mad when your child seems not to hear your pleas for action of any kind. Even when they are looking straight at you! You can see their eyes zoning out. It follows that taking direction of any kind is often problematic. What they are listening to needs to float their boat! Not be 'boring'. So, things that are a bit tedious to them need to be broken down into short soundbites to have any hope of them being taken in. Possibly sandwiched between something they find really interesting.

Organising. Planning. Prioritising. To be able to have a realistic career idea and be acting on it, you need to be efficient with all these three skills. Such a complex task for the ADHD brain. A key area of career coaching that will cause huge issues if not carried out in some way.

Beginning a task and completing it. Simple for those who don't struggle with their executive functioning but almost impossible for those who do. Being able to focus on that journey from beginning to end... nope! Such a gargantuan task.

Taking on board other points of view & ideas. To be able to do this you need to be able to listen for long enough and focus on something that is different from your own narrative. Just for a minute. Jump from what you think to understanding the view of another.

Keeping control of your emotions. Oh yes, those emotions! The reason that the young person in front of you goes from calm to furious in a split second. Happy and cracking jokes one minute, in floods of tears the next. So difficult. So challenging for most teens wrestling with puberty but for an ADHD young person, you need to batten down the hatches. Not worry too much when the emotions before you take a rollercoaster ride. Expect that they will.

Keeping track of things (inc. time, belongings, plans already made etc). So, your ADHD teen has found themselves with no plan having left school and it seems like a shock to them! Time blindness is the reason amongst others. Believing you have loads of time to think about something but never do. Or losing track of the plans and ideas you started to hatch a couple of months ago. Or losing the notebook that you made the plans in.... yep, you get it.

It is no wonder that they need your support to help organise and plan their future. They are unlikely to be able to do it alone. It doesn't mean that they are lazy, or they have a low IQ. The exact opposite. There are so many thoughts and feelings that they are overwhelming. They need you to support the executive functioning part of their brains. Put some scaffolding up around it! Take the weight. It's worth it. They are worth it. You believe this too as you are taking the time to read this book. You can be your child's Career Coach and I will show you how.

From my many years' experience as a Careers Adviser, and parent, I have identified the nine main issues that are making life impossible for your ADHDer when moving from one key stage to another. These same issues affect any major decision that they will make in life not just career choice. I also accept that the same issues impact any adolescent when making decisions. But for a teen with an ADHD diagnosis, or traits of, it is turbo charged in its level of difficulty.

I also acknowledge that ADHD often doesn't stand alone. It can be joined by comorbidities such as autism, dyslexia and dyscalculia to name a few which also have an impact on the ability to formulate a clear career plan. I'm concentrating on ADHD for the purposes of this book as I have experienced firsthand the disruptive nature of this condition.

We'll have a look at each issue and examine how it looks. How do you know that it is an issue for your teen? How does it present itself? What on earth can you do to help?

I have worked with teenagers from age 13 right up to age 25. My focus has been age 16 to 19 unemployed young people. This has involved picking up the pieces when things go wrong. Fresh perspective. Supporting parents to see what I can see. Helping teens move forward with a level of confidence that has so far evaded them and with a spring in their step.

Research tells us that there is a link between an ADHD diagnosis and being unemployed. I don't want your teen to be at crisis point. I really don't want them to be unemployed and disillusioned. I want to help you with the skills you need to ensure that they don't get to this stage. But if they do find themselves confused and feeling that they don't have a bright future... I aim to show you what to do. Don't despair! It will be ok.

You just need to understand what the difficulties are and what is going on in that complex brain. Then you can help and support in the right way. No amount of discipline, consequences or atmosphere of tension in the house will help. You don't need to tear your hair out as I will explain what is going on and how to deal with it!

Before I do, here is a list of what your teenager is NOT:

- Lazy
- Stupid
- Unambitious
- Apathetic
- Truculent
- Useless
- Doomed!

Yes, they probably **appear** to be all these negative things... but look again. Your ADHDer is struggling with a condition that affects future planning massively. The executive functioning part of the brain needs support. This is your cue to help it out.

Unemployed young people will often have an ADHD diagnosis or at the very least traits that are getting in the way of moving on successfully. I have seen so many distressed parents dragging their child to see me. I have tried to persuade some out of cars while Mum or Dad is red in the face with embarrassment and anger! Some are dropped off by the door with threats of what will happen if they don't 'sort it out'. Some come nervously themselves with parent's irate voices in their ears... "Please write it down so I can prove to my Dad that I've been."

It is also important to say here that in my experience ADHD is more often than not genetic. So, the reason that you are so anxious and upset by your teen's inability to progress is probably because you struggle yourself. But that is a book for another day. Do some research...think back to when you were the same age. Did you have similar issues?

I have watched whilst war breaks out between parents and teens. I have attempted to cool things down so we can start to create a way forward.

The lucky ones have a concerned adult by their sides. An adult who has tried everything to help and doesn't know where else to turn. These are the adults that are willing to learn and understand and are worth their weight in gold.

With the right approach, it is possible to support your own ADHD teenager into making a decision that is right for them.

Chapter 2
Where Do I Start?

So, this book is about supporting your child through a really difficult process to make a realistic and informed decision.... wow that sounds challenging, doesn't it? It is but I'll tell you how.

Choose your Time Carefully

Choose a time when you know that your young person is at their most receptive. This could be an hour after they have had their ADHD medication for some, or when they are feeling good about themselves after playing their favourite sport...etc.

You will know the right time but pick wisely. You don't want this to turn into a confrontation. The last thing you need is for the accusations to start flowing and then the whole subject of their future becomes stressful and a no-go area. If communicating is impossible then this is when you need outside help. A careers adviser or an ADHD coach can help. The novelty of an 'outsider' is sometimes what they need. If this is the case, don't feel discouraged. It can be helpful to get someone else's perspective, and professionals can help you turn the dialogue into a more positive, encouraging tone and then you can carry on the good work.

Communicate Calmly

It's important to take notice of the way in which you are communicating. This includes not only your tone of voice but also your body language.

Your voice needs to be at your normal conversational pitch. Use humour wherever you can and don't be too serious. ADHDers usually have a brilliant sense of humour so use it to engage them and let the conversation flow. Resist the urge to turn on 'teacher mode' as this will get you nowhere. You may just see the back of your teenager as they exit the room and slam the door...! Try to keep it light. If you really can't or it is just not a good day...please give up for now. If you don't think your teen is feeling it, give up for today.

Your body language is also vital. Your teenager will pick up on your nonverbal cues as much as the verbal. A trait of ADHD is a high capacity for empathy and the ability to read people quickly. So, try not to look tense with a tight expression with your legs and arms tightly crossed. Never point or wag your finger! You know your child best. How do they feel most comfortable chatting to you? Sometimes this can be side by side not looking at each other. If this is the case, do it! If they want to lie down on the sofa, let them. It is ADHD we are talking about so it maybe that they need to jump about, lounge on the floor or sit upside down. Whatever works…just go with the flow. Don't panic and imagine how will they ever cope with a job interview. That isn't what you are trying to achieve here and believe me they know what the difference is. They won't act in the same way in a formal environment so don't try to mimic it…unless they love roleplay of course.

Don't get all formal and chat to your child across a desk. This just acts as a barrier to your conversation and will alienate them. Your aim is open and comfortable dialogue. A chance for them to talk about what they really think and what matters to them. A desk just creates awkwardness and can also act as something to hide behind, so they don't have to engage.

Time Limit

If communication can progress, then you need to set a time limit with your teen. For example, "Let's have a chat about careers for 30 minutes.' You can even put an alarm on so that they know that it will end, and it may well help focus the mind.

It is essential to break any 'careers chats' up into short chunks. The ADHD brain will not enjoy long winded lectures of 'back in my day'! This means that it is best to plan what you are going to talk about for those 30 minutes. Share this with your teen and agree what you need to talk about beforehand.

Explain that you have 30 minutes today to cover as much as you can. If you don't cover everything you will come back to it another day. ALWAYS leave your ADHD teen wanting more. The 30-minute slot sounds realistic and hopefully won't put even the most severe ADHDer off.

Honesty

I would let your teenager know that they can be honest and open in their chat with you. Tell them that they can express any views that they want and promise not to share your opinion with them. Reassure them that it is about them and their ideas and feelings not yours. Tell them that you won't judge them or try and talk them out of their ideas. You MUST stick to this! If you have had disagreements about future plans before, you must agree that you are making a fresh start. That you are putting any previous conversations behind you. Open your mind to their thoughts and feelings and promise yourself that you are there to listen and not lecture.

If you feel that this is an impossible task in your relationship, then please get the help of a professional. You will do so much emotional damage if you are not prepared to really listen and let your teen explore their thoughts and ideas freely. There may be issues that are brought up that you don't agree with, but you mustn't let this show.

A Contract

In other words, make a list with them and share what you want to cover. I will share with you what your contract may look like in the Tool Kit at the back of this book. Keep your explanations to a minimum. Most ADHDers have speedy brains which can get to the point of things very quickly. They don't need you to go round in circles about how you are trying to help them and why. You don't need to tell them how important it is that they listen and concentrate. Believe me they have heard this so many times before it will just wash over them!

In my experience, a written contract works wonders. Write down some bullet points of what you think is important to discuss and then share it with your child. Ask them if they agree and/or want to add anything. I find written contracts work much better than verbal as they can be brief and understood quickly without the risk of going off at tangents and wasting your precious 30-minute slot.

Ask your child which bullet point they would like to start with. E.g. your bullet point could be 'school subjects'. This would be a conversation about which subjects they like and why. Which subjects they don't like and why. It's a great ice breaker and gets them thinking about their likes and dislikes and more importantly the reasons behind their preferences. Get them to tick each one off as you cover it.

After the 30 minutes is over, you **must** stop! Don't be tempted to carry on if it's going well as you risk boredom and frustration setting in. Finish by summarising what you've been talking about and let your teen tick it off on your written contract.

Questions

Right, so now we are into the questioning style that works best. Remember this book is all about helping your teen reach a complicated decision but in a stress-free way. Unfortunately, ADHD and anxiety can go hand in hand. Don't add to this by ramping up the tension. This means that you shouldn't have a list of pre-prepared questions to read out and expect an answer to. You are following the contract that you have agreed at the start, so you have a loose plan. Let your child choose the subject as above and go with it.

As a Careers Adviser, my rule of thumb is the 80/20. This means that your young person should ideally be talking 80% of the time and you should only speak for 20%. Your job is to start off the discussion and guide them towards their own decision. If this doesn't happen don't worry. You are not expected to have the skills of a professional just by a quick read of this book.

To help you get anywhere near the 80/20 rule, you need to use mostly open questions. So, what is an 'open question'?

An open question is one that encourages your child to answer in their own words and not with just a yes or no answer. An example of an open question could be,

"What kind of music do you like?"

OR

"What do you like most about English?"

OR

"What didn't you enjoy about your part time job?"

It encourages discussion and helps your young person to open up with a fuller answer. This then gives you more insight into their feelings and ideas. It can make your chat more engaging and help it take a deeper direction. The key point for ADHD is that it will make your child feel that you are genuinely interested in what they think and feel. You will also be more able to judge what stage they are at with their career planning and whether you do need to seek professional support to help them catch up.

Open questions can be sandwiched around some short & snappy closed questions. So, what is a 'closed question'?

A closed question can be answered with a 'yes' or 'no' or a brief statement of fact, for example:

"What mark did you get in Maths?"

OR

"Did you enjoy your work experience?"

OR

"Are you OK?"

Closed questions can be useful if you want to concentrate on facts rather than feelings. Or if you want to clarify something that your teen has said e.g. 'did you mean....' They can also help to keep a conversation brief so if you have an ADHDer that likes to chat and ramble on a bit (many do) a closed question can be used to keep the discussion on task.

Summaries

Your verbal summary needs to be done quickly and agree to write it down for them so that they can come back to what you have discussed without having to talk to you again if they don't want to! Remember short and snappy is the way forward with ADHD. Your 30 minutes is up so don't keep going back to it throughout the day as that will just irritate and break your agreement– unless you are asked a question of course. But even then, keep it short. Don't go into a full-blown lecture as it will put them off asking again! Just answer the question.

Write a summary of what you have talked about but again use bullet points where you can. Your child won't take the time to read through long paragraphs. Don't be tempted to add more into the written summary. It just won't get read and serves no purpose.

Agree Actions

After each 30-minute slot, it is crucial to agree on some action points for you and your teenager to carry out before your next chat. This again should be bullet points and give you both a task to bring to your next 30-minute slot. The types of tasks could be:

1. 'Mum to ask Aunty Sue if Josh can go into work with her one day to see what she does'
2. 'Josh to go online and research teaching in more depth'

In this way it focusses your discussion and gives the feeling that you are working together. Ask your teen what your action points should be ready for your next chat and tick it off your contract once you have decided.

Don't have lots of action points as this can be overwhelming and demotivating. If it's too complicated, it will just get sidelined and won't happen. You will then find yourself frustrated at your next meeting which takes the wrong atmosphere into the discussion right at the start. You know how it will go,

"So have you found out about teaching?"

"No" grrrrrr!

Action Plan

An action plan is simply the summary and the action points above put together. It gives it a title and somewhere to write those all-important action points. An example of an Action plan is in the Careers Tool Kit at the back of this book but remember that you are dealing with ADHD here. Make it brief but make sure you capture what was said. One of the reasons for using 30-minute discussions is that it doesn't cause information overload.

Where you record your action plan is also key. You will know how your teen likes to work. Is everything done on their phone or laptop? If yes, use messenger or emails to record the information. It's informal and serves a purpose. Your teen may prefer notebooks and will like the idea of having one just for their career planning. Get them to choose the style of it and go with their interests if they want e.g. a football team cover etc.

So, let's move on to the key issues mentioned previously. You will find that some of the nine key issues overlap and intertwine with each other. Just like the structure of the brain! It is very rare that your teenager is being affected by just one issue, rather a complex mass of issues. However, there is usually one or two that stand out and are causing the most problems. Identifying what they are is key to supporting your teen to come out the other side.

Let's look at what the problem is...

Chapter 3
Key Issue Number 1 Procrastination

What is it?

In a nutshell, procrastination means delaying doing something. In the case of career planning, putting off making that decision. Delaying starting to think about 'the big question' i.e. "What do you want to do when you leave school?"

Procrastination is a key symptom of ADHD. The main reason for this is that the sheer volume of internal thoughts & feelings alongside outside distractions leaves very little room for pondering the future.... especially if it doesn't really interest you at the moment! It can be genuinely difficult to get started even if you really want to.

What does it look like in your ADHD teen?

Most adults know what procrastination feels like. The feeling that you need to start some DIY, but you would rather watch a game of football. The feeling that the house needs cleaning, but you have a more interesting phone call to make! Sometimes inventing things to do...and I mean anything.... to avoid the more difficult/boring job!

This is a perfectly normal behaviour, however, like most issues relating to ADHD it can be turbo charged and therefore, chronic. Multiply your feelings of procrastination by 100....

With your ADHD young person, there are clues that you can look out for that prove procrastination is a problem with their career planning.

You will know by now how they approach homework and exam preparation. Do they rush it just to get it done and over with OR do they just never start it! If they are in the second group, you probably have a procrastinator on your hands.

This can apply to any task really. When you request that their room is tidied, do they do it at great speed and often badly to get it over with.... or do they never start?

The reasons why your teen is procrastinating is due to their ADHD. But what is it in particular that they are finding difficult?

Thinking about what they would like to do with the rest of their lives is huge. The non-procrastinator will be happy to make a snap decision and give things a go (this too can cause problems eventually. The ADHD procrastinator will struggle to start even thinking about it.

The reasons for this are that nothing feels interesting enough to motivate them; or the feeling that they will be no good at anything anyway; or that they don't want to voice what they think for fear of being made fun of…so it's easier just not to dwell on it.

Whatever the reason is, it needs addressing for your young person to move forward. They are avoiding the issue which will eventually impact their lives.

What does it look like in career planning?

Brain Fog:

The first observation may be, when you ask the 'big' question, they are unable to think of any type of job or career area at all. They just don't know what on earth to say. They wear a blank expression that makes you think they have never come across this question before. Their body language can also appear anxious. Wringing of hands; playing with a piece of their hair; biting their nails; looking away. You may also find big silences ensue. Not just short stop gaps…. but HUGE silences that seem to go on for eternity! No amount of waiting time will give a response. They may start to look anxious and awkward. Blushing and possibly even walking away. Remembering something urgent that they must do that you feel that you can't argue with e.g. revising for that difficult chemistry exam…

The Butterfly:

The second way that you can spot an ADHD procrastinator is the inability to commit to any one idea. So, they will seemingly engage with you but have a huge list of job types. I call this young person the careers butterfly.

They flit around mentioning all kinds of things. Even talking at length about the aspects of one job just to then throw another one into the mix. You think, 'fantastic, my boy is really thinking about his future', only to find that he never actually settles on one thing. The types of careers mentioned can be many and varied and have no relationship to each other. There is perceived safety in this for your ADHDer, as if they never settle on one idea, they never actually have to DO it! This reduces the chances of humiliating themselves as they feel that they won't be good at it anyway. (Don't underestimate this one…lack of self-belief in ADHD is **massive**.) It also postpones the boredom of trying to motivate themselves to actually crack on and commit to it. Working towards relevant qualifications, gaining some work experience, or even completing an application form.

This works for your young person as it really does throw you off the scent for a while! As a parent you don't really realise what is going on until it is too late to do anything about it. Deadlines have been missed, precious time to focus on specific qualifications needed has been wasted.

Lots of ADHD young people seem to have excellent verbal skills. If this is the case, they can be superb at being the butterfly. They can tie you up in knots with their reasoning around each job type. Discussing pros and cons eloquently only to jump onto something else in a split second. As a parent trying to help them reach a decision, it is exhausting trying to keep track of that fast and complex brain. You quickly reach saturation point and go and make a brew instead. It makes you feel frustrated and a little confused. Win/win for your teen!

Even as a professional Careers Adviser, I find these types of young people extremely challenging. Your interviews can run massively over the allotted time as, yet another idea is thrown in just as you are writing up your list of things to do next.

The Mind Changer:

The final observation I have of the ADHD procrastinator is the big mind changer! This young person will go all in on an idea. They will complete the applications; go along to open days; do the research and attend interviews relating to a particular career. They will tell EVERYBODY about their wonderful plans and how excited they are. They will almost appear like they are riding the crest of a wave. They are sorted and shouting it from the rooftops. As a parent you are so relieved and satisfied that a seemingly realistic decision has been made. It seems achievable for your teen. You allow yourself to relax.

Then, slowly but surely, you begin to hear some negatives coming out of your ADHDer's mouth. Some 'what if' questions about their choice. You begin to develop a seed of doubt that the big idea is no longer such a sizeable one.

They start to literally talk themselves out of it. Their concentration jumps from the positives to the negatives of their choice. They appear anxious and confused. They reject whatever aspect of the once favoured job you mention to them. Within a couple of weeks, they are lost again.

As a parent this can be really depressing. The feeling that you are back to square one when you were so nearly there. The emotional investment in visualising your child thriving in the chosen career only for it to be whipped away is difficult. Especially if you find that this happens several times. You begin not to trust it and help support the idea less. "They will only go off it so what's the point in helping."

This situation is hard to recover from. Especially if it happens numerous times. But recover you must. No matter how many times this happens. Hopefully each time will help your teenager to see the pattern of their thinking needs to change just a little. You can assist them in this...... so, deep breath and keep moving forward. It is all part of career planning with ADHD. Don't feel foolish in front of friends and relatives. It really doesn't matter what Joy across the street thinks when she finds out that Lilly has changed her mind again.

So how can we help?

Now we've had a look at what your ADHD teen's procrastination with career planning looks like, we need to know what on earth can we do about it. Lots of the reasons for the procrastination are deeply rooted in low esteem and poor self-belief. ***Research tells us that by the age of 10, on average, children with ADHD receive a full 20,000 more negative messages than a child without it.*** Not only do they receive a disproportionate amount of criticism, but they are also probably more sensitive to it. The upshot of this is that they instinctively avoid situations where they may be criticised or humiliated. They are more likely to either do nothing or choose the easier option.

Their difficulty being able to focus and concentrate on certain tasks will also buy into their belief that they are not as good as others. So, procrastinating about 'important' stuff is a shield against the harm that it not working out can do to the fragile ADHD ego.

We also now know that the sheer boredom of tasks needing sustained mental effort, prove impossible to your ADHD teen. Procrastination is useful to combat this too!

Your child is not being lazy or disinterested. It is just that career planning is **so** difficult for them.

Slow it down: Some of the solutions for this are as simple as **slowing it all down**. Expect it to take longer for your teen. Take the pressure off you and your child. Accept that their condition means that this key transition period will take a little longer while they mature emotionally.

You cannot expect an adolescent with a diagnosed (or undiagnosed) neurodevelopment condition to progress as if they hadn't got it. Let your friend's kids travel along their own path. It probably won't be without bumps in the road. Don't compare and become disillusioned if it is. Your teen will get there. But for now…SLOW IT DOWN! If you put unnecessary pressure on, you will increase the procrastination as anxiety levels will increase.

Your child will need so much reassurance that they will get there. Believe me they do not need you to reinforce negative feelings by comparing them with others. They feel it so intensely themselves. They need to understand that most people make decisions in life that are wrong at one time or another. Tell them about when you made the wrong turn yourself and put it right. Tell them about your niece who went off to university and realised that she was on the wrong course and in the wrong place for her. Tell them about where she is now and prove that although it felt dramatic at the time, it was all ok in the end. Show them that life is all about twists and turns.

Research some famous people with ADHD (and without!) who have navigated their lives around obstacles and wrong decisions. Argue that decisions are never really wrong ...just part of a road to get you where you should be. Your teen needs kindness and support. They need understanding of a condition that makes decision making really challenging but not impossible. Reassure them that you are there to catch them when and if they fall.

By doing this you will reduce some of the feelings of fear attached to procrastination and avoidance in ADHD.

You can support your teen to reduce the anxiety about making decisions by actively 'doing' rather than just avoiding thinking about career planning. The idea is that you then make situations less fearful, so procrastination is reduced.

Use your contacts: A useful task to do as a parent at this stage is to sit down and note all your contacts that are approachable. Jot down what jobs they do. Put a star by those that you think that could chat to your child about their work.

You can then go on to ask those contacts if your teen can come and talk to them for 30 minutes about their career and a bit about how they got there. If you can ask them to throw in a bit about any wrong decisions and how they sorted it out, so much the better.

Mini Work Experience: Having looked at your contact lists and chosen some of them for your teen to talk to, which people do you think may be able to offer your child a morning's work experience with them? Longer if possible? But a couple of hours should do it. It doesn't really matter what the job is. By getting your ADHDer out there watching and chatting to real life people in real life situations so much the better. It will help to remove the mystique about what a career is and help them realise that making decisions is just part of everyday life and that people change career paths all the time. If you have a contact that has changed their career choice …fantastic! If you have a contact who is ADHD too even better!!

Reward: So the above suggestions are great. But what if you have a teen who is resistant to even chatting to another adult human. Not uncommon. Motivation struggles and social anxiety could mean that they say nope to your helpful suggestions. In fact, you may get major procrastination to avoid something that they would find so uncomfortable. One of the answers may be reward. You could put some treats in place if the 30-minute chats and mini work experiences are carried out. Reward really helps motivation for ADHD brains. Choose things that they are really into and that you know that they will struggle to resist. Or agree to a 'bonus' to their usual pocket money. Whatever fits with your budget but you will find it is more likely to be received favourably if rewarded.

Body Double: Body doubling in ADHD is all about having another person present at a task or situation that you find difficult. The person doesn't even need to be actively involved in the task but needs to be with you…to sit alongside you as a kind of 'anchor'. It helps in lots of ways. It can make the task more fun if you have a companion with you. It can reduce social anxiety as you have a friend there too. It can make you less distracted as a body double can help keep you on task. A body double can be anybody! So why not have a think if your child has a friend who would benefit from some chats with your contacts and some mini work experience. Their parents will probably be pleased as it will benefit their teenager too. Be creative. Think about how you can do this.

Voluntary Work: Being a volunteer may help your teen become less fearful about the workplace and realise that they can contribute successfully to an organisation but in a low risk way. You may need to use the reward and body doubling strategies above to get them started though.

PROCRASTINATION: AN EXAMPLE

Adam

Back Story: Adam was diagnosed with Inattentive ADHD in primary school. His parents identified his struggles early as they have an older child who is also diagnosed. He received loads of support at primary and high school as his main issues were around keeping on task and not getting distracted.

His behaviour was always fine, and he had 2 close friends that went to the same high school with him. Adam was described as rather quiet and sometimes anxious in school. He struggled with overthinking decisions but always had someone there to help. He benefitted from some good one to one support in the subjects that he found came less easily to him. He was also on medication that suited him and had help with homework & revision.

Luckily, one of the learning support staff he worked with was a close family friend which led to Adam engaging well and feeling comfortable.

Adam went on to do well in his GCSEs and passed all nine with good grades.

He was supported by his parents and school with his next step and the feeling around his future was a positive one.

With help, Adam applied for an engineering apprenticeship that he felt interested in at a large organisation within easy travelling distance of his home. He also applied for a course at the local college as a backup.

Things continued to go well for Adam as he beat huge amounts of competition to be offered the apprenticeship, and he was also offered a place at college on the course of his choice.

Adam left school and was suddenly away from the supportive environment that he was used to. Although his parents tried to help, he missed the security and routine of school. He continued to see his 2 friends but learned that they were going to a different college to the one he had chosen as his back up option. This led to Adam starting to feel very anxious about his future for the first time and the procrastination raised its head.

Although he had started to have some doubts, he decided that he would choose the apprenticeship route as people kept telling him how well he had done to be offered it. He began to get lots of emails and letters about the apprenticeship with detail about training and start dates. Adam for the first time learned that the initial training would involve being away from home for 4 weeks.

At this point, Adam completely changed his mind about the apprenticeship. Although he was still interested in engineering, he felt that he couldn't go on the 4-week residential training. He came up with many reasons why this was the case and turned the apprenticeship down.

His parents became angry and frustrated with him. They just couldn't understand why he had turned down a golden opportunity. Adam felt he couldn't cope without his support network and became fearful. He had become very reliant on the help that had been put in place for him and began over thinking what may happen without it. He also struggled with using public transport on his own and was worried he wouldn't get to places safely.

Adam chose to go to college on his chosen course as it felt safer and more suitable for him. Support was agreed for him but was poor in comparison to that supplied by his high school. He attended college until Christmas but then refused to go back in the new year. He said that he had changed his mind about his course subject and that he was not able to make friends.

How to turn it round

Slow it Down: Acceptance that the transition needed to be slowed down. Adam's emotional maturity needed to grow. So, taking a gap year was key but making sure it was filled with useful experiences.

Prioritise: Adam needed support with prioritising his ideas and deciding what is important to him.

Mini Work Experiences: initially with family & friends to build his confidence and generate fresh ideas.

Public transport practice: with family as this was something he had never had to do.

Driving lessons: to increase his feelings of independence.

Voluntary Work: in a local foodbank, charity shop & farm with a friend as a body double. Reassurance that if he changed his mind about one it was ok as he always had another.

Research: Loads of support carrying out some careers research to broaden his ideas.

References: Obtaining positive references from his work experiences & voluntary work to increase his self-esteem.

RESULT

Adam realised that he didn't enjoy a full-time college course as he liked the flexibility to work alongside it. He decided to take a more academic part time course at a different college that kept his options open. He was able to get a part time job with one of the contacts that he had made in his gap year which he was enjoying too. This enabled him to buy a car of his own so that he could feel that he could go home after lectures. He felt more in control in this way.

This delayed Adam having to decide on a plan that he felt he had to stick to for the rest of his life and kept the procrastination to a minimum. He realised that he could keep his options open and work towards a career that would suit him better. This in turn reduced his anxiety and levels of procrastination.

PROCRASTINATION: NOTES

Chapter 4
Key Issue Number 2
Boredom

What is it?

Well, we all get bored I hear you say. Just find something to do! The age-old cry of the child who wants to be entertained rather than actually finding something to do.

Boredom can be defined as the brain being insufficiently stimulated or engaged by whatever is going on in the environment around it. It can lead to feelings of frustration and irritability.

As with all the issues I'm focussing on, with an ADHD brain the feeling of boredom is extremely intense. Imagine the general feelings of boredom and then multiply it. Boredom in ADHD can indeed cause feelings of frustration and irritability. But also, restlessness, fatigue, lethargy, numbness, impatience, anger, depression and even sometimes be physically painful and uncomfortable.

It is possible that people with ADHD need higher levels of stimulation and become bored more easily. This is probably due to their reduced dopamine levels. The upshot of this is that the ADHD brain needs higher levels of excitement & novelty to keep it on track and focussed so boredom is a very real issue.

What does it look like in your ADHD Teen?

This one is probably easier to identify than most. However, it is also the one that is easily dismissed as non-ADHD related. Let's face it, all teenagers and children have periods of time when they appear bored.

In your ADHD teen it will be a state of mind that you see probably daily. If not daily, it will hang around frequently.

Your child may just mooch around the house doing nothing in particular whilst hunting for that dopamine fix to stimulate that bored brain. The hunt may result in:

- eating huge quantities of snacks
- sniping at you or siblings just to get a reaction
- restless movement from one activity to another

- throwing household objects around
- throwing themselves around physically
- emotional distress such as crying & appearing low
- appearing anxious or panicky
- indulging in risky behaviour such as jumping off things that are dangerously high
- lying on the sofa or bed for huge chunks of time
- aimlessness

If your teenager takes themselves off out and about when they are bored, very risky behaviour can then ensue. The use of drugs & alcohol can temporarily reduce their boredom. As can getting involved in gambling, fighting etc.

It is, therefore, crucial to find ways of controlling and reducing this intense ADHD symptom as it can result in devastating conclusions.

There is research that also suggests that intense ADHD boredom can happen after a period of hyperfocus and success. If your child has had a fantastic period of engagement in something e.g. a role in a school play, the chance of a period of boredom leading to depression when it finishes is extremely high. This is because the clarity that comes with hyperfocus cuts through the mental noise and muddled thoughts that are usually there in ADHD. When the hyperfocus ends, there is a high likelihood of an emotional reaction until the brain is stimulated and engaged once again.

If this is a pattern that your teenager struggles with, then you need to be sure to prepare for it and support them to do this. So, if the hyperfocus has been preparing for a presentation at a job interview, you need to work with them to ensure that that they have something engaging in place for when it finishes. You may find resistance in this but hopefully with maturity they will be able to see a pattern emerging so that they can go some way to helping their own mental health in the future.

I could go on and on at length about boredom in ADHD but the focus of this book is to be able to support your child with their future planning... so let's re focus!

What does it look like in Career Planning?

From the descriptions above it is clear to see how difficult boredom can be to deal with for ADHD teens. When we throw career planning into the mix, it's easy to see how things get sticky.

Avoidance: The first way that you will be able to tell that boredom is playing its part for your child is AVOIDANCE.

Your ADHDer may have no idea about what they would like to do when they leave school/college and just avoid doing anything about it. Any conversations about the future are met with stony silence or an argument.

Or your teen may profess to know exactly what their plans are...but have done absolutely nothing about it.

Either way this is so frustrating for a parent and there are multiple reasons at play. Rest assured BOREDOM is one of them!

The whole process of planning what you want to do is just too BORING! They cannot motivate themselves to start to do anything about it.

Their assumption will be that to research jobs you need to read loads of books. Then once you have done that you need to decide which qualifications you need. Once that is done, which route to take. College, apprenticeship etc?

When that is decided the application forms and interviews kick in. Then when you have done all that, you have to start something! It is so much easier and more comfortable to avoid and act like there is nothing pressing on the horizon.

It is just not stimulating or interesting enough for you to start to engage in it.

The Butterfly: The second way you can identify boredom in career planning is a teenager who jumps from idea to idea, but nothing seems to stick. You may get a flicker of interest and think that you are on to something before they are on to something else. We saw this with procrastination too. The reason for the indecision this time is that your child cannot think of a job that won't bore them. The anticipation and fear of boredom prevents them from focussing on a career that would stimulate them enough to be successful.

Boredom in ADHD can be so intense that having a fear that it may happen is enough to avoid thinking about it altogether. The assumption that all jobs are boring means that you don't have to pick one and find out more about it.

How can we help?

Acceptance: As with the earlier issues, the first step to helping your ADHDer with boredom is to accept that it exists for them. Not only accepting that it exists, but that in ADHD it can be a real problem as it is felt more severely and more often than for a neurotypical teen. Whereas an adolescent without ADHD can just pick up a book to entertain themselves, it is highly unlikely that this will distract your child for very long even if they can pick it up at all.

Remember that the idea of planning your career can appear just too boring. An idea that starts in your mind but can quickly impact your body and emotions too. Just thinking about a career plan can make their mood plummet.

To be able to support your teen with career planning you will need to help them control the feelings of boredom. A few suggestions that may help are:

- **Hyperfocus**: Go with whatever their interests are as a starting point. For example, if their current hyperfocus is football, support them to research jobs connected to football so they can feel motivated enough to start. There are all sorts of jobs connected to the industry that they won't have thought about so it can spike some interest in something unexpected.

- **Mix it Up:** set aside an hour a day for career focussed activity. Whether it's some online research or an application form to college. But ensure that it is framed by something more exciting at the beginning and something stimulating at the end. For example, you could encourage them to start by using an online game or interest guide that is loosely related to career planning. They can then jump on to their video game of choice as a reward when they finish so that you are sandwiching the boring bit in the middle!

- **Timer**: set a timer to spend an agreed period on something career related. A time limit and watching it tick away gives a sense of urgency and excitement. For example, "see if you can do this job application in 30 mins!"

- **Podcasts or Music**: allow your ADHDer to use background music or whatever engages their brain. I know it seems like this would be a distraction, but some ADHD brains have the ability to focus on many things at once. It may, in fact, help them to focus and concentrate on a subject that they don't feel is terribly interesting to them.

- **Use your Network**: do you have a friend that is really engaging and can talk to your teen about their job? If they can exude enthusiasm and excitement about what they do it will prove to your child that jobs can be fun.

- **Reward**: reward is highly useful in ADHD. So, you can use it as a bargaining tool. "If you get your college application in, we can order pizza." Whatever works!

- **Media**: use the gloss and excitement of film and TV to help your ADHDer learn about the world of work. Suggest films that are related to a career that you think may appeal to them.

- **Equipment**: let them have some stationary that they love or maybe use Dad's expensive laptop to research jobs or complete boring application forms. It may just stimulate the brain enough to be able to progress.

- **Body double**: as discussed in an earlier chapter, having somebody with you whilst trying to complete boring tasks can work wonders. So, suggest a friend comes round and they can plan together…but chose the most sensible child you can think of.

BOREDOM : AN EXAMPLE

Jay

Back Story: Jay was diagnosed ADHD in primary school and displayed all the characteristics of hyperactive type. He had always been described as a 'lively' boy who struggled to listen. His needs were met at this level as he was able to engage in play like education which included lots of activity breaks for him to burn off his energy. Jay is one of twin boys whose brother is neurotypical. This contrast always made Jay stand out even more as having struggles and difficulties.

Jay began having more problems after starting secondary school. He loved to be active and there just wasn't enough of it to stop his ADHD brain becoming bored and under stimulated. Although he had one to one support thanks to his early diagnosis, Jay found it excruciating to sit still for very long. The expectation of this level of education is around sitting down and listening to a teacher in most cases. Jay just could not achieve this as his brain craved physical activity to keep it stimulated.

Jay stopped attending school and preferred to be out and about on his bike and kicking a football against a wall. Teachers and parents tried to get Jay back into school but although he did try for short periods of time, he soon opted out again. School attempted to give Jay more physical activity breaks but even this didn't do the trick. He had simply become bored with the whole concept of school and resisted it with all his might. He was fed up with the same building, the same teachers and the same kids. He was fed up with people trying to get him to sit still and listen to them.

As his final leaving date approached, Jay's parents put an application into the local further education college on his behalf. They chose a construction course that they thought would keep him active enough to reduce the boredom. He had left school without qualifications and so unfortunately would be expected to do the basics of English and maths alongside his construction course.

Jay spent his summer on the go! He would ride his bike for miles with a friend or on his own if his friend wasn't available. It didn't seem to matter to him. He was happy enough in his own company. His parents were concerned as they often were unsure where he was but understood his need to be physically busy.

He began his college course reasonably enthusiastically. The novelty of a new environment and new people enabled him to start well. However, within a few weeks of the new routine things began to get difficult for Jay. The same pattern emerged as the course just wasn't active enough for him. The expectation that huge chunks of his time be spent in classrooms just reminded him of school. His brain became bored and craved stimulation in other ways. Jay stopped attending college. His course tutor sent a letter home to say Jay was no longer on the course.

Jay's parents were really concerned and didn't know how to help him. His twin brother was already racing through his A levels with a concrete idea about his future in place. The contrast was baffling to them. At this point, a family friend suggested Jay get some help in the careers centre.

How to turn it round

Acceptance: boredom is a very real and painful issue for Jay…both emotionally and physically. It isn't Jay just being lazy and not open to thoughts about his future. He just cannot think of anything that doesn't make him feel bored or the feeling that the thinking about jobs is just too boring. Jay needed to be supported in a different way.

Humour & Activity: He was encouraged to arrive at his initial appointment on his bike. He brought it into the office with him and the adviser spent 30 mins chatting to him about cycling and used humour. Jay then went home with the feeling of a short and snappy positive interaction.

Short appointments: His second appointment was similar but the idea of planning for his future was introduced at the end. He was happy to attend as he knew it was short and he could ride his bike there and back. He also knew that he enjoyed talking to the advisor. An enjoyable experience for Jay that kept him stimulated.

Mix it up: the adviser arranged the third appointment at a coffee shop that did great milkshakes that he knew Jay loved. The location was also far enough for Jay to be able to get a good bike ride in there and back. The discussion touched on Jay's interests and future ideas for the first time, and he was also able to extend the time to 45 minutes. He was given a bullet point action plan of a couple of things to think about before his next session.

Reward: He was rewarded with a milkshake!

Body Double: The fourth appointment was back at the careers centre and Jay was encouraged to bring his friend with him. He enjoyed showing his friend what he had already done about thinking about his future and told the adviser that the only thing he enjoyed doing was artwork. He liked drawing tattoo art and showed some photographs of examples of what he had done on his phone. He was able to decide that although cycling was fun it was really just a way of getting his energy levels out. The discussion then was about how long it took him to produce this art and what environment suited him best etc. The action plan for his next session could then look different and have some real purpose for the future.

Hyperfocus: By the fifth session which again took place in the milkshake/coffee shop, Jay was able to feedback that he had ridden his bike to a local tattoo studio and asked about an apprenticeship. This was an enormous achievement and shows what hyperfocus can do. Jay had found something he was really interested in and was now determined to do something about it.

RESULTS

Although the tattoo artist couldn't offer Jay an apprenticeship, he did offer him a day per week work experience. He was really impressed with his designs and said that with some more experience he may be able to give Jay some paid work. Jay was delighted and started spending time at the shop every Monday…cycling there and back.

He also decided that he would go and study a part time art course at a different college to improve his drawing and design skills.

Jay is now spending his weeks doing both things and has a real plan for the future in place that enthuses him. He no longer escapes on his bike but still uses it as his main mode of transport. The tattoo studio owner is impressed with his commitment and passion and has offered him an apprenticeship starting the next academic year.

By reducing the boredom of planning a career, the adviser was able to get to what Jay's true passion was.

BOREDOM: NOTES

Chapter 5
Key Issue Number 3
Self Esteem & Self Belief

What is it?

So, this is a huge issue for most ADHD people. Large numbers will struggle with this, and they are often the ones that you just wouldn't suspect of feeling doubtful about their own abilities.

How we value and perceive ourselves has an impact on every life decision and transition point. These feelings are usually deep and often hidden. They are based on opinions and beliefs that we have developed about ourselves, sometimes over many years.

As mentioned earlier, the ADHD child will have heard many more negative comments aimed at them than average. Even the innocuous,

"Can you pay more attention...?" is harmful when you feel that you are really trying to but just can't.

"You must try harder"

"Just concentrate"

"Stop talking"

"Stop fidgeting"

"You are just weird"

"You don't listen"

"You are so annoying"

"You are so rude"

"You say stupid things"

"You are in a world of your own"

"You are too loud"

"You are stupid"

"You are irritating"

"I don't want to be your friend anymore" etc.

The repetition of these kind of remarks creates a negative mindset in our ADHD teenagers. They are often followed up by punishments and 'consequences' for their behaviour or lack of effort. They wear away at self confidence in a child who is already struggling to fit in and is trying harder than most.

By the time puberty hits, a high proportion of our ADHD teens will have chronically low self-esteem and belief in their abilities and strengths. They believe that they must be flawed as it has been reinforced by almost everybody they have encountered. Parents, teachers, friends, relatives. Harmful and destructive remarks that are taken to heart.

Most ADHD teens are very, very sensitive to criticism. They remember the bad stuff and store it away. It will revisit them, and they will play a negative soundtrack in their minds which leads to such poor levels of self-confidence.

For young people that have such busy brains with so many thoughts and feelings, you can appreciate how many times these negative comments pass through. Round and round again like an over played song. Attaching themselves to worries for the future and self-destructive thoughts.

ADHD can also come with high sensitivity to rejection. I'll cover this in a later chapter but, for now, it's enough to know it exists. Rejection Sensitivity Dysphoria (RSD) means that even the mildest put down or failure will result in strong reactions for your child. Shame, guilt and panic are among the negative emotions that they are likely to feel. Some even describe it as a physical pain.

Self-esteem and self-belief can also be eroded in our teenagers by problems with friendships and relationships throughout their childhood. Difficulties with schoolwork and studying which have been unsupported so they will feel that they are less able than they are. They also may have struggled with the stigma that an ADHD diagnosis can still give. All topped off with the perceived perfection of images that they see on social media. A toxic mix for any teenager but ADHD makes this so much worse.

What does it look like in your ADHD teen?

Your child may have become really withdrawn. The once loud and rumbunctious small child will be quiet and wear an unhappy expression. They will appear self-conscious and almost look like they would prefer to shrink from view.

This in my experience, is a form of self-protection. The less 'out there' they are, the less they will be noticed. The less notice people take of them, the less negative comments they will hear. The less hurt they will feel. Complexly, they may appear extra loud and hyperactive in situations where they feel more comfortable. Behaviour may become difficult to manage as risk taking increases.

You may find that they will assume that they will never be much good at anything. That there is no point considering any exciting future plans as they will never be able to achieve them. They may believe that they will never be as successful as their peers so what is the point in trying.

Your child may also really struggle to come up with any of their strengths. They believe that they don't have any, or, if they are brave enough to voice them, that they will be ridiculed. In my experience, this peaks in high school combined with the delights of the increase in hormones due to puberty. As a parent this can be a very worrying stage. It is devastating to watch your once confident child struggle with such difficult feelings. Especially when you know how wonderful they are. It makes you want to wrap them up and keep them from harm. However, if you try and do this you will probably be on the receiving end of some really bad 'teenage' reactions. Eye rolls and door slams will be on the mild end of this! They are likely to react irritably and prefer to be alone while they try and process difficult feelings.

I don't want to make light of this issue as it is one of the most distressing impacts of having ADHD in my opinion. It can also lead to poor mental health and all the problems associated with that. If you are concerned that your child may be struggling with severe anxiety and/or depression, please seek medical help. I will also include some useful links in the Careers Tool Kit.

The reassuring news is that maturity does help. Your child will be able to see that they do have a role and are good at lots of things. Their confidence will build as they start to gain more positive points of view from the people around them.

What does it look like in Career Planning?

This young person can appear self-conscious and nervous from the outset. However, they can also come across as confident and chatty. In my experience as a Careers Adviser, judging an ADHDer's self-esteem and confidence levels can be difficult. This is because ADHD teens are highly practised at masking. Masking is something I will look at in a later chapter as it is such an important part of knowing where your teen is up to emotionally.

As a parent, you will definitely have the advantage over a careers professional with this one. This is because you will know your child better than anyone. You will understand their body language and facial expressions. You will be highly skilled at identifying a turn of phrase that your ADHDer uses when deflecting from the serious conversations. Trust in how well you know them from having raised and nurtured them for so many years! You will know when they feel uncomfortable about an idea or when they are just trying to appease you by saying what they think you want to hear. Your teenager will find it impossible to mask at home all the time…especially when they are emotionally exhausted through having to play a part all day. Hopefully this will mean that you get the real them.

However, your teen will probably find it difficult to identify strengths about themselves for all the reasons described above. They will wear a blank expression when you ask them what they can do best or come out with set descriptions that they have read that you know don't really apply to them.

Another way of identifying low self-esteem is the inability to imagine themselves in any kind of job scenario. When using some open questions (as discussed earlier) your teen will be unable to react positively to any type of career. They genuinely believe that they do not have the ability to succeed in any role.

This will particularly apply to anything that involves working with the public or large groups of people in any way. They show interest in jobs that are 'behind the scenes' but are unable to articulate why. You can check out their feelings by asking some closed questions such as:

"Is that because it would make you feel embarrassed?"

"Is it because you think that you'd be too shy to do that?"

You may also find that your child will have come to the decision that they are just not as able as their peers. When you ask what a friend is interested in doing as a career, they will tell you and follow it up with

"…but I could never do that"

Again, they will struggle to give you reasons why and you may just get a shoulder shrug.

They may tell you that their friends are going to be doctors, engineers, teachers, and then follow this up with a lower skilled/lower paid job for themselves. Now this is fine if that is the career that suits their personality, and they are genuinely interested in it. However, you may find that your child is under valuing themselves and is terrified to say anything different due to ridicule and poor self-worth. A number of ADHD teenagers that I have worked with have named a job and then when asked why have said

"…because it's easy"

They may also name a job that they have some experience of due to a placement at school etc. This is because they know what it entails and feel some level of confidence that they could give it a fair go.

My experience has shown that lots of ADHD teens will assume that they need to be able to 'do the job' straight away. They have difficulty in acknowledging that you need to train and learn things step by step. This can be part of inattention as they struggle to see the steps that they need to get through. They naturally focus on the end result without the planning and training it takes to get there. This leads to overwhelm and sometimes task paralysis as explained in a later chapter. It just seems too big and too scary and someone like them won't be able to do it.

How can we help?

- **Strengths & Weaknesses:** to be able to have any direction or plan we need to support our ADHDer to work out what their strengths are and also their weaknesses. There may also be a middle group entitled 'work in progress' or something similar. This task is a Careers Adviser's bread & butter, but you can do this successfully with your own child. Just remember the 30-minute chunks of time as described earlier and also catch them at an appropriate moment. Keep the humour and no long lectures! It is a good idea to start with the weaknesses list as your teen will unfortunately know this better and find it easy to reel off. Don't disagree for now. Just get some words down…. You can then reverse things and get them to identify their strengths. This will be more difficult as we are probably dealing with someone who has low self-esteem and belief, but getting the weaknesses down first should help. For your next chat, you can work with them to discuss each strength and weakness and maybe swap them around to different lists with the help of your opinion. Tread carefully as ADHD teens don't like being told what to do so 'guide' rather than 'tell' if you can. If this develops into a heated debate you may be better leaving it for another time or getting a professional involved. Don't make their future ideas a no-go zone. Try and reinforce their strengths and celebrate them. Reassure them the weaknesses don't always matter and that everyone has both. Show them that there will always be aspects of jobs that they will find more difficult than others, but they can work towards or seek help in certain areas. Leave the chat on a high with positives swirling round their brains!

- **Identifying jobs**: you don't have to do this yet! Identifying strengths and weaknesses is a huge job and a definite step in the right direction. Leave them to ponder on it for a while and give them time to research some careers that interest them with their new knowledge. It will also give you some idea of where your child is re self-esteem. If the strengths list is severely lacking, then maybe you need some outside help.

- **Cognitive Behavioural Therapy (CBT)**: Cognitive Behavioural Therapy is well used in ADHD and can be very useful. Due to all the reasons described above, your ADHDer may have developed some negative thought patterns and hold negative beliefs about themselves. Some professional help regarding this is so useful to challenge their thoughts and help them realise that just because they think something it doesn't mean that it is true. You can find a link to finding a therapist in the Careers Tool Kit at the back of this book.

- **Small Steps**: Learning to take small steps is key to supporting the organisation skills of the ADHD brain. Alongside this, self-esteem is automatically improved as once perceived overwhelming things are ticked off and a light at the end of the tunnel can be seen. It is such a simple thing for neurotypical teens to do but for ADHD teens it can be an impossible task. By learning to take small steps to achieve things, it is possible to see that they are attainable and that you don't have to complete everything at once. This, in turn, improves self-belief. An idea or an interest is enough to start with.

- **Volunteering**: Teens with ADHD will compare themselves to their peers all the time. They will assume that that everyone else is so much better than them in every way. By getting them out volunteering you will be changing their environment and enabling them to mix with different age groups. School can be a pressurised & toxic place where they feel constantly judged. Hopefully this will increase some self-confidence by proving that they can function successfully in a different environment.

SELF ESTEEM & SELF BELIEF: AN EXAMPLE

Bobby

Back Story: Bobby was diagnosed with ADHD while in primary school as he was viewed as 'different' from his peers. His behaviour at this point was quite challenging and he was considered to have Combined ADHD showing hyperactivity and inattentiveness. With puberty, Bobby became very quiet and emotional. He was medicated for high school and so was able to focus more on his studies and went on to achieve excellent GCSE grades. He was described by school as 'no trouble' and just 'got on with it'. Bobby's parents felt that he had become 'almost invisible' in school which was a contrast to his years in primary school as a younger child.

Bobby's high school was a short walk from his house, so he was able to get himself there without many issues. His sleep pattern had always been difficult with him lying awake for hours and then being difficult to wake up in the morning. Although this did impact a little on his school attendance, he managed to get in most of the time and continue to achieve.

Having gained good grades, his mum and dad enrolled him at a local college for a higher-level course and chose for him as Bobby couldn't think of anything that he wanted to do. His parents were frustrated with him as he seemed disinterested in everything.

Bobby started a computer course at college as his parents agreed that he must like it as he spent so many hours gaming!

He started college reasonably positively, but his parents noticed that he seemed quite withdrawn and sometimes close to tears. By the Spring term, Bobby was struggling to get his work in on time and complete assignments. His attendance had slipped, and his sleep pattern was proving disruptive.

Bobby's parents spoke to the college to see how they could help him, and Bobby was supported to get his outstanding work in. By the start of the next academic year, Bobby was refusing to go back to college.

He found the college too big, and he hadn't been able to make any new friends. He said he hated his course and didn't like computers anyway!

Bobby's parents were at a loss so asked him what he would prefer to do. He couldn't identify anything that he wanted to do and felt that he wouldn't be able to do achieve.

How to turn it round

Alternative options: The first step was to reassure Bobby that alternative options were available to him and to accept how well he had done so far with the lack of support in school & college. This took the pressure off him as he could not envisage himself going back to college. He was relieved and more positive about looking at other things.

Strengths & weaknesses: Bobby needed to explore his strengths and weaknesses which was quite a difficult task for him as by this stage he was feeling low and had poor self-esteem. By identifying his weaknesses first, he was able to see what strengths he had, and which were real things that he could work on rather than negative thoughts.

Bobby felt that he would prefer to continue in a work-related way so was keen to look at apprenticeships and job vacancies. He agreed to attend a job search session once a week.

Voluntary Work: Bobby began some volunteer work in a children's farm as he had always loved animals. He was able to do afternoon shifts which he found easier to get to in case he struggled with his sleep. This took some pressure off him and made him realise that he could do something and was respected by the farm owners.

RESULTS

After a while, Bobby was successful in gaining an apprenticeship in a warehouse where he could work late shifts and wasn't public facing. His confidence increased as he received positive feedback from his employers, and he completed his apprenticeship quicker than anticipated. He was offered a permanent position and enjoyed the feeling of reward that being paid gave him. Bobby's self-esteem improved significantly.

SELF ESTEEM: NOTES

Chapter 6

Key Issue Number 4
Rejection Sensitivity
Dysphoria (RSD)

What is it?

RSD is not a formal diagnosis but does tend to appear alongside ADHD. It usually presents as intense feelings and emotional sensitivity in response to perceived rejection or criticism. It can be long lasting, extreme and feel unbearable.

Emotional dysregulation is one of the most difficult parts of ADHD in my opinion, and feelings are heightened anyway. It makes sense that any form of rejection is then felt intensely. If you add this to the hormone activity our teenagers are going through in puberty, then things can get heightened.

What does it look like in your teenager?

Any teen in the midst of puberty can feel hurt and disappointed by not being included or feeling rejected. For example, the breakup of a relationship; being dumped from a friendship group; not being included in the football team, criticism from a teacher etc. This is seen as the normal but painful route into adulthood!

In our ADHDers, however, these feelings are huge and can last for long periods of time. The kinds of emotions to look out for are:

- Extreme emotional outbursts after something that is usually deemed quite minor. This could be upset and crying or anger and lashing out…or both.
- People pleasing behaviour to avoid any future rejection. ADHD teenagers will do anything to fit in with their peers as they have usually experienced rejection more than most.
- Completely withdrawing from a situation or relationship after an incident that they have seen as rejection.
- Going over and over past rejections either out loud or silently
- Avoiding any future situation where rejection may be possible.
- Always feeling like a failure before even starting things

- Over defensive to criticism of any kind. Holding a grudge when constructive criticism has been given.
- Perfectionism. If unable to complete something 'perfectly', they will give up and possibly never try again.

Rejection sensitivity is not something to be taken lightly and can be extremely painful for your ADHDer. It can have an impact on lots of areas of life including employment, education, and relationships. For the purposes of this book of course, I am going to concentrate on what RSD does to planning and securing a future career.

What does it look like in Career Planning?

Starting to think about a career path is a big thing for a teenager. It involves imagining yourself in a totally new scenario with unfamiliar people and thriving at it. In fact, doing so well at it that an employer is prepared to pay them for their trouble!

Now, try to envisage yourself as a 16-year-old with ADHD. You are a people pleaser by nature as you have had to do this to fit in during your years of education. You are unsure whether you will fit in anywhere new and feel very self-conscious. Your gut feeling is that you won't be very good at anything anyway due to your low self-esteem (see earlier chapter). You are bound to do something wrong and then be criticised for it so is it best to just ignore it and don't give it any thought?

When your ADHD teenager moves through the hurdles that education brings and into the job market, rejection is par for the course. The job interview is so challenging for ADHDers as rejection is inevitable at some point. This can also include apprenticeships, university or anything that has a selection interview. The anxiety beforehand to either radio silence or rejection from the employer is just dreadful for them. Imagine how this triggers the overthinking and the anxiety. Followed by a huge dose of RSD!

Below are the ways that ADHD teenagers can behave when affected by RSD in career planning:

Avoidance: Some teenagers with ADHD will just do nothing. They will form a very high proportion of the youth unemployment figures (See appendices: Research) These young people are commonly described as lazy but the majority aren't. They just avoid the possibility of so much hurt and negativity by opting out of applying for anything. If they don't put themselves out there, they won't get rejected…simple.

Low expectations: As well as avoidance when RSD is evident in career planning, you may see low expectations. Choosing a pathway that is not a reflection of true potential cushions the ADHD teen from hurt. Opting for the 'easy' route. They may say things like "I could never do that" or "that's too difficult for me." They may set their sights far too low for their ability. This can continue into adulthood by being too fearful to push for promotion in case rejection is experienced. Rejection sensitivity can prevent ADHDers from reaching their potential in case they expose themselves to possible humiliation and hurt.

Procrastination: There is an earlier chapter on procrastination, but it pops up again here. Indecision and being unable to decide on a path forward can be due to rejection sensitivity dysphoria. The 'can I or can't I' is about taking the risk and putting yourself out there for possible rejection.

How can we help?

Slow it Down: With so many of these issues that impact ADHD teens with career planning, this one appears again and again. If you slow the process of deciding on future plans down, you reduce the pressure and anxiety that makes RSD worse. I have included a biological age versus the executive functioning age of the ADHD child in the appendices so take a look. There are no rules about when your offspring is the 'correct' age to move forward. It may be that they are more able to cope with rejection with a little more maturity so let them develop. Ensure that they are doing something positive with their time and wait it out.

Mindfulness: There are lots of anxiety reducing techniques out there online that can be useful for rejection sensitivity. One of these is **The Pause.** If rejection is suddenly felt intensely……take 10 seconds. Accept that the intense feeling is because of the ADHD and then re-evaluate. Helping your teenager to acknowledge and understand what this feeling is helps.

Lower the Risk: Use your networks and try and get your teen some mini work experience placements as described earlier. By getting them used to going into work environments in a no pressure way, anxiety will lessen and they can make some potential connections more casually. A potential opening may even come without the stress of an interview. If not, you are reducing the fear of rejection by introducing them to employers who know you and will hopefully be supportive.

Support Network: Help your ADHDer identify the feelings that are RSD and to act when it happens. Encourage them to build their own support system of people that they trust whenever they start to have feelings of rejection. Trusted relative/friend, teacher, careers adviser, or even yourself. Let them know that it's ok to reach out and say, "my RSD is kicking in!" A few calming words from somebody that they trust will help reduce the anxiety and remind them why they feel so intensely.

Cognitive Behavioural Therapy (CBT): If your teen is really struggling with the effects of rejection sensitivity, don't hesitate to seek professional help. A professional in CBT will be able to help make the negative reactions and thought patterns a little easier to cope with. See appendices to some links to organisations who can help.

REJECTION SENSITIVITY DYSPHORIA: AN EXAMPLE

Mo

Back Story:

Mo had never been diagnosed with ADHD or any co morbidity when he came to see me. He had struggled through school with poor attendance and high anxiety levels. He felt unsure why this was other than he couldn't motivate himself to get himself there and found it boring.

He managed to get good GCSE results even though he was "hardly ever in school." He was unsure how really other than doing some very last-minute revision which caused him enormous stress.

Mo started 6th form where the same pattern began to emerge. He had been so looking forward to a fresh start and just being able to focus on the subjects that he was interested in but began to lose interest after the initial novelty of a new place.

He was asked to leave due to his attendance and missed deadlines which was a shock to him. He felt very hurt and rejected and that his teachers thought that he was not good enough and just wanted to "get rid" of him. He couldn't understand why the college hadn't just allowed him to carry on as he had in school. He felt that they thought he was "not very bright" and felt extremely emotional about it.

Mo appeared very down when explaining this and told me that his parents had high expectations of him and didn't understand why he couldn't just attend and do well. He said that he agreed with them and felt that he would never be able to do anything that was worthwhile. He told me that he had investigated alternatives as he felt a bit lost and under pressure from his parents to find a job.

He had been successful in getting an apprenticeship interview with a travel company that he felt quite excited about. He felt that the interview had gone well but that the employer had called to say that he had been unsuccessful. The employer had said that although he was unsuccessful, he had done well, and they would be in touch as a more suitable role for him was coming up.

Mo had felt so disappointed and was convinced that the alternative role had been mentioned to let him down gently. He said that he felt the employer thought he was 'stupid' and so he had blocked the number.

Mo was now unemployed without a career plan and feeling very low in confidence.

How to turn it round

Explaining RSD: by explaining what RSD is, Mo began to realise that his feelings were real but that his reactions were out of proportion and why he had felt them intensely. We talked about why the 6th form college had an attendance target and that it was no longer compulsory education like school had been. We also discussed the travel agency company and how it was a positive thing that they had said that they would be in touch. I supported Mo to give the company a call (after unblocking their number). He was invited in to have a chat with them about a new role that they had the following week. We talked about how to cope with his emotions if he wasn't successful.

Voluntary Work: I supported Mo to apply to do some voluntary work with animals as he adored dogs. He went for a 'no pressure' interview and was offered some hours at weekends at the local dog rescue. This boosted his confidence and he felt better about the interview process and realised that he could be successful.

Cognitive Behavioural Therapy (CBT): I talked to Mo's parents about cognitive behavioural therapy and how this could help in the future. Mo's Mum understood and remembered that she had felt rejection intensely at his age. She supported him to talk to his GP and also bought him a short course of CBT where he felt more able to identify his negative thought patterns around rejection and his reactions to them.

Pursue ADHD assessment: after understanding what ADHD is, Mo was able to identify traits and symptoms that he felt he struggled with.

He felt that he would talk to his GP about an assessment at his next appointment.

RESULT

Mo succeeded in getting an apprenticeship that he loves. He attended several interviews and coped with the roller coaster ride that is job search. His apprenticeship is with a local charity where his role is to help organise events. Mo is thriving and feels that his new position is the right one for him and was worth the wait.

RSD: NOTES

Chapter 7
Key Issue Number 5
Masking

What is it?

Masking is the term used when somebody plays down or hides their symptoms of ADHD or in fact, any other condition. This is common in people with ADHD and can be done purposely or subconsciously.

It is extremely common amongst teenagers as the need to avoid judgement from others means that traits and symptoms are hidden.

Masking can be exhausting as there is constant worry about appearing to stay organised, censoring impulsive reactions, and any other trait you can think of. Teens are desperate to fit in anyway but if you add a condition like ADHD in, things can get difficult. Living with ADHD can be challenging enough, and masking can cause overwhelm and anxiety just by the effort of constantly having to do it.

What does it look like in your teen?

The teenage years are probably the period in life where blending in is most important. Most teens naturally want to belong and be liked. ADHD teens will almost always have memories of feeling ashamed about some of their behaviour as a child. They will remember being judged negatively at some stage and so will know what they must do to stop this happening.

Your ADHDer will show their masking behaviour in lots of ways. Here are some of them:

- Trying to copy an individual or a group of teenagers who they feel don't have ADHD. This can mean copying speech; likes; dislikes; mannerisms and forcing themselves to be just like them
- Trying to copy a celebrity to appear socially acceptable. For example, dress sense, language, confidence
- Arriving too early for situations such as school or social events and finding it hard to relax.
- Excessive note taking so that nothing is forgotten.

- Appearing fine and bottling up emotions. Then extreme emotional outbursts when they are back in their safe place.
- Appearing totally different at home to how they appear in the outside world. E.g. loud at home and very quiet at school.
- Using substances such as cannabis and alcohol to fit in but to also try and control racing thoughts and busy brains.
- Exhaustion & fatigue at home after hours of holding emotions and behaviours in place.

What does it look like in career planning?

Masking when attempting to discover which career path is the right one for you is problematic. It will without doubt lead to an unhappy time at work. To be able to consider what you what like in a job, your ADHD teen needs to unmask. This means dropping all the defence mechanisms and coping strategies that have been so carefully built up over the last few years. Difficult!

Your ADHDer may say that they are interested in a career that you are amazed by! This is often because as parents we see our children without the camouflage that they use for the outside world.

They may come up with a career idea that someone in their peer group is interested in. An example of this could be a role in computer technology. You know that your teen struggles to sit still and is at his most content when he is active so you cannot imagine him in a corporate office environment. Needing to be still and focussed for long periods just doesn't seem to fit your hyperactive child!

You doubt yourself and feel that maybe you don't know them as well as you thought you did. Perhaps they have matured into someone who could do this without you noticing! However, deep down you know that your teenager is masking his interest in this career so that he can imagine himself as somebody without the challenges that he struggles with.

In my experience, masking during a careers guidance interview can look like the teenager is calm, collected and organised. They appear as if they are ready to pursue the job that they are waxing lyrical about!

The truth is that they are often hyper focussing on masking and will be exhausted afterwards.

The same is true for job interviews. They are often able to convince an employer that they are perfect for a role that will potentially lead to exhaustion and burn out.

Your ADHD teenager may appear very anxious when trying to consider their next steps. If they are masking about their job ideas to teachers, friends etc it can create anxiety. They will probably experience some self-doubt about what they can do and become confused about the skills and strengths that they do have. What is real and what is made up?!

They may appear to have difficulty with over planning and excessive checking of details to do with career progression and different jobs. This may be in an attempt to mask their difficulties with their ADHD symptoms.

Your teen may be masking to colleges, universities and employers through fear of being thought of negatively due to their ADHD diagnosis. This is probably due to the stigma and misunderstanding that they have felt in the past. They would rather mask than benefit from any useful accommodations that could really help due to the judgements that they have felt.

How can we help?

Communicate: you are probably one of the only people that sees your teen without their mask! This is an honour as you can clearly identify what strengths they truly have but also what they struggle with. The tricky part is discussing this with them. Remember the 30-minute rule I mentioned earlier and pick your moment well. Short and snappy is best and explain what masking with ADHD is. Once your child can understand when they mask and when they don't it is easier for them to identify their strengths and weaknesses.

Self-Awareness: knowing what your strengths and weaknesses are as a teenager is incredibly difficult. Your support in this can be key. You can use the techniques in earlier chapters but also try and get your child to see scenarios where their mask would be 'thick' and where it could be 'thin' as they would feel more comfortable to be themselves. This whole process will help them to recognise when and how they mask which is crucial for the development of a fulfilling career path. Try writing three columns. Entitle one 'Mask' and another 'No Mask'. You can also have a middle column. Support your teen to put the environments and/or situations where they mask in the correct column as they see it.

Strategies/Accommodations: Help your teenager to come up with some examples of scenarios where they do mask. For example, in a particular lesson where the teacher makes them feel anxious. Help them to understand why they feel this way and what would make them feel better about the lesson. Perhaps they are pretending that they understand the subject but are really struggling to concentrate. Speaking to the teacher on a one to one would help draw up a plan that would enable them to cope better and feel confident that the teacher is on their side.

Maybe they mask heavily with a certain group of friends. Discuss the reasons why they feel they need to and how they can cope without masking. Remember that this means your child must talk about their true feelings and this makes them vulnerable. It could be incredibly difficult for them. Be patient.

Support: As conversations about masking can be really challenging, they may not want to feel exposed and talk about it with you at all. If you think that this is the case, but masking is having an impact on what they would like to do in the future, consider getting some outside support. It may be crucial to help them to avoid unhappy working environments or jumping from job to job. Look out for an ADHD savvy Careers Adviser; an ADHD Coach or therapist that would work well with your child.

MASKING: AN EXAMPLE

Ffion

Back Story: Ffion came to see me for careers guidance having completed high school with average to high qualifications. She told me that she had an ADHD diagnosis and had dyslexia but had coped really well in school. She appeared very confident and self-assured.

As our discussion progressed, Ffion told me that she was struggling with anxiety and had recently left an apprenticeship at a local estate agency.

She told me that she had always been 'loud & chatty' and the 'life and soul of the party'! Her Mum, however, recognised a much deeper and very sensitive teen who often shut herself away for hours.

Ffion told me that she felt that she was just not the type for studying and wanted an apprenticeship when she left school. Her main group of friends were keen on reality TV shows and in particular the real estate programmes! They had encouraged Ffion to go down this route as she was just like the girls in the show! Ffion was flattered that they thought this and so went along with it.

She went on to successfully get an apprenticeship with an estate agency who had quite a 'cutthroat' reputation for hard sell. The employer felt that her gregarious and outgoing personality would be perfect for them, and everything was great for the first couple of months. Ffion got on well and was a fast learner. She was quickly given more responsibility, and the employer was delighted with her. As well as coping well with her new position, Ffion made sure that she was up really early in the morning so that she could spend time ensuring that she looked like the girls she had seen on TV. This image of success was important to Ffion and she put huge effort into achieving it.

However, after this initial period, Ffion began to feel exhausted. She steadily became later getting into the office until one morning she couldn't make herself go to work. She was anxious and depressed and didn't understand what was wrong with her. Why was she feeling like this? She had the perfect job that suited her really well and yet she felt as though she had no energy left.

Ffion felt that it must be the employer that didn't suit her and to try somewhere different. She went on to successfully get two more apprenticeships in the property industry one after the other. The same pattern emerged, and Ffion was left unemployed and feeling a failure when things didn't work out.

She just didn't understand why she couldn't cope when this job was perfect for her on so many levels.

How to turn it round

Explanation of masking: by explaining to Ffion what 'masking' is and how it can come together with an ADHD diagnosis, she began to see that this was exactly what she had been doing. She had been trying to fit into an environment that didn't suit her and that meant that she had to wear a mask in order to cope. Exhausting.

She also realised that she masked with her group of friends so they didn't know the real her. No wonder they had encouraged her to pursue a career that was so wrong for her! She had gone along with it all and ended up in the wrong situation. Explaining to Ffion that this level of masking can cause severe burn out made her realise how important her health is.

Strengths & Weaknesses: Once Ffion had allowed herself to drop her mask, she was able to start looking at her true strengths and weaknesses. She felt that she didn't enjoy the sales environment where she had to play a part to be successful. She realised that she wasn't the outgoing confident person that she had portrayed. She was empathetic, caring and sensitive. She enjoyed looking after people but was also comfortable in her own company.

With support Ffion also worked out that she had masked by not disclosing her ADHD or dyslexia diagnosis to her employers. Useful accommodations and strategies could have been put in place to make her experience much more comfortable.

Slow it Down: She developed a genuine interest in a career in nursing as this was a way that she could be her more sensitive self and the environment felt right. Having thought that she didn't want to continue in education, she felt keen to go to college. She now knew that there would be support for her conditions and that she could work towards a nursing degree if she wished. She could enjoy her course and take her time deciding what the right career path for her actually was.

RESULT

Ffion is at college studying Health & Social Care. Although she still has her challenges she feels well supported and is enjoying the subject. She is looking forward to seeing where this will take her and she is far less anxious.

MASKING: NOTES

Chapter 8
Key Issue Number 6
Social Anxiety

What is it?

Social anxiety is not just a case of your ADHD teenager being a little 'shy'. Social anxiety is a real condition that commonly occurs alongside ADHD. Its symptoms can include extreme self-consciousness, fear of judgement from others and panic attacks.

It can lead to avoidance of social situations and isolation. Some people with ADHD who struggle with social anxiety are very outgoing in situations that don't trigger their actual worries. Reactions can be extreme and cause difficulties in every area of life.

Social anxiety can be one of the most difficult parts of ADHD and feelings are heightened anyway during puberty.

What does it look like in your teen?

Social anxiety usually comes from the fear of being rejected, humiliated or judged negatively in social situations. If you put ADHD on top, then the worries about how you are perceived by others are more intense.

Your teenager may worry that their ADHD symptoms will make others dislike them e.g. zoning out of conversations; missing the point; butting in; being too loud etc. These probably will be the types of things that they will have been made aware of socially before and they have felt uncomfortable and hurt by.

Unfortunately, this can then lead to avoidance of social situations or events where there will be a group of people that they don't know. Feeling that you are annoying to others makes it easier to take a step back and stop engaging rather than face the judgement and rejection that is likely to come. There are a few ways that you will be able to tell that your teen is struggling with social anxiety alongside their ADHD. They may:

- start to miss parties or social events
- appear lonely and /or disappointed

- appear very emotional and have meltdowns
- struggle to ask a teacher for help even when they will get in trouble if they don't
- avoid answering in class, reading aloud or giving a presentation
- struggling to get to sleep or excessive sleep
- irritability
- changes in eating habits such as overeating or not eating enough
- withdrawing from family gatherings

These types of behaviours can be easy to write off as just 'normal teen stuff' but feelings will be more intense and consequences of negative emotions more extreme.

If you think that your ADHDer has a level of social anxiety, keep an extra eye on them as substance misuse, self-harm etc can occur as a way of trying to escape painful feelings.

What does it look like in career planning?

Job search and career planning is anxiety inducing stuff for everybody! Putting yourself out there to potentially be rejected is not enjoyable. For our young people it can be horrific and can result in:

Avoidance: for your ADHD teenager the prospect of judgement and scrutiny can be just too much. As ADHD can co-exist with poor self-esteem and rejection sensitivity, it is simple to see why it is easier to opt out. They may just refuse to engage in any conversation about the future. They may just shut down or walk away. They may become irritable every time it is mentioned until the subject becomes too difficult to bring up again. It's crucial to remember that your child is not being rude or disrespectful. They are avoiding an issue that they see as potentially doing them harm. Your teen is anxious about it so 'fight or flight' kicks in.

Low Aspirations: Your teen may become fixed on a career idea that requires less entry requirements & lower financial reward than they are capable of. No matter how hard you try you cannot raise their aspirations. You are so frustrated as you know that they are not going to achieve their potential with this option.

The answer is that they are just too socially anxious to consider a career that better suits their ability as it will mean that they are wide open to judgement and criticism by people. If it is a career idea that they are truly interested and invested in it will hurt too much. If they settle on an idea of a job that they feel that they can do easily, they will feel that the risk of humiliation is less. This will then make your teen less anxious as there is less at stake…less skin in the game!

Paralysis: Your teen may want to look at a future career path and feel excited to do so. However, when it comes to applying or attending interviews their fear of judgement, criticism and possible rejection just won't let them go any further. They get stuck and can't move forward. This can appear lazy and disinterested. It isn't. It is social anxiety getting in the way.

Copying: inability to think about what they genuinely want to pursue as it is emotionally too high risk. It feels too uncomfortable to put themselves out there so following a friend or family member is a safer path. There is security in feeling that if it works for somebody you know well then it could work for you too. It feels safer to have a friend with you for the ride doing the same thing or following a parent/sibling into a career that is comfortable with a network already in place. This is fantastic if their aspirations genuinely match their own. However, in the case of our ADHDers, there is a strong possibility that they are impacted by social anxiety and just cannot follow their own path. A friend's choice feels safer as there is less emotional investment if things go wrong.

The disadvantage of moving forward like this is ending up in a job or career that is unsuitable for your teen. It has the potential to cause much stress, unhappiness and possible burn out in the workplace.

How can we help?

Slow it Down. There is no rule carved in stone that suggests that all young people must progress at the same pace. Having an ADHD brain means that your child will think differently, and their executive functioning skills will be approximately 3 years behind their neurotypical peers. By forcing decision making and pressurising them to move into colleges, jobs etc with new people will create more anxiety. By allowing them to mature and getting involved in nurturing activities during a gap year, their confidence will grow. Take the pressure off and reduce the social anxiety. 'Slow it down' appears in most of the issues having an impact on our ADHD teenagers and in my experience is the key to successful progression into a meaningful career.

Lower the Risk & Use Your Contacts: use your networks and try and get your teen some low risk, mini work experience placements as described earlier. By getting them used to going into work environments in a no pressure way, social anxiety will reduce, and they can make some connections more casually. A potential opening may even come without the stress of an interview. Reach out to your family and friends who your teenager is familiar with. This reduces the fear of judgement about meeting new people. It will help to broaden their outlook and build their confidence.

Explain: by explaining to your child that social anxiety is common emotion when you have ADHD, it will help them understand why they feel this way. It will help them to identify when it happens for them and the things that trigger it. It should reduce the shame that they feel by admitting that this is something that they struggle with. You can help by encouraging them to do something small that takes them out of their social comfort zone once a week. This will help develop their confidence. For example, if your child is avoiding replying to a message from a new friend due to being too socially anxious, support them to do it. Small, low risk wins will help them to see that they can push through this feeling and good things can happen.

Cognitive Behavioural Therapy (CBT): If your teen is struggling with the effects of social anxiety in a big way, don't hesitate to seek professional help. A professional in CBT will be able to help make the negative reactions and thought patterns a little easier to cope with. It is important for them to realise that there is help and techniques that work to help them to move forward.

SOCIAL ANXIETY: AN EXAMPLE

Holly

Back Story: Holly was diagnosed with ADHD when she began struggling with her mental health in Year 9. Although she was always considered to be bright, she was often described as being 'too quiet' and 'not joining in' class discussions. One teacher even described her as seeming to be in 'physical pain' when she was asked a question in class.

Holly began to withdraw from her group of friends, preferring to spend time alone in and outside school. This was a change in behaviour for Holly as she had always felt comfortable around her small group of friends. However, she just stopped communicating with them. After a while, they stopped asking her to go along to things which left her isolated.

Holly received an ADHD diagnosis and tried medication. Although this did help her focus during lessons, her social anxiety increased, and she started to avoid school altogether. Her parents were confused as they assumed ADHD was about not being able to sit still and concentrate. They felt that once Holly was on medication she should be able to cope with school much better.

Due to her poor attendance, Holly was transferred to alternative provision. This was a smaller school environment where Holly's struggles were well understood. After a stressful settling in period, Holly began to do well and feel more comfortable. Class sizes were small, and she could spend time in a breakout room if she felt overwhelmed. Her attendance massively improved and she was able to make some new friends. She remained extremely quiet but seemed to cope much better.

Holly managed to pass some GCSEs with good grades but opted out of some subjects totally. She excelled in the subjects that her friend was taking too, and they could study together. She appeared more confident in these subjects.

She began to think about the future and her aspirations increased. She was keen to continue with her education and loved to study.

At the point I met Holly, she had received better than expected exam results and was keen to apply for higher level qualifications at a local college. We explored a couple of different colleges as Holly was struggling to accept that one of them wouldn't accept her as their entry requirements were too high. She also wanted to go there to be with her friend.

I worked with her to look at other options even though they didn't feel as 'safe'. Holly was able to broaden her mindset and became interested in an alternative college that was in the city centre and farther away from her local area. This was a big jump for her, and we discussed the issues around this decision. Holly's Mum felt concerned that the change was too big, but she was keen to try so I supported her with her application. We carried out some preparation work together to prepare her for the change as the college in question was a large city centre campus and Holly didn't know anybody else who went there.

Holly started the course well and managed to do well in some tests and seemed to be making new friends. However, a couple of months into her course, Holly suddenly stopped attending and her anxiety became very severe again.

Holly and Mum came back to see me, and we discussed what had happened. The big change had all been too much for Holly and she now realised that she was overwhelmed by the amount of change and new people. She had started to feel 'too quiet' for her new friends and that she wasn't very interesting. Her social anxiety increased as she became more self-conscious and worried that she just didn't fit in. She felt disappointed and worried that she would never be able to study again.

How to turn it round

Explain: explaining social anxiety to Holly. By explaining what social anxiety is, Holly realised that this was part of her ADHD and was common. She also began to understand that most young people struggle in new situations however, her ADHD made this feel worse for her.

Virtual Study: as Holly had been open to trying a big college environment but this had proven too overwhelming, I made the case to the local authority that being able to study from home would ensure that she would succeed. Her social anxiety would decrease making her more able to focus on her studies and enjoy learning again. Holly felt that this was the right route for her at the moment and her parents were delighted that she could feel comfortable enough to achieve.

Voluntary Work: I supported Holly to apply to do some voluntary work within a charity shop. She was really interested in fashion and the idea of retail but felt that getting a job in a shop would be impossible for her. She went for a chat with a contact of her mum's whom she already knew and started to do a couple of hours work in a local charity shop. This boosted her confidence, and she began to really enjoy it. She started to easily chat to customers and began to realise that she could be successful in jobs that involved people.

Cognitive Behavioural Therapy (CBT): Holly's mum felt that she would benefit from some cognitive behavioural therapy alongside to help reduce her social anxiety. She was waiting for a place to begin this but was already feeling more positive about working on her worries.

RESULT

Holly completed her virtual course and gained excellent grades. She began to spend lots of time in the charity shop and became involved in stock display and helping at other branches. She decided that she would enjoy a job in the retail industry and was successful in gaining an apprenticeship with a leading fashion brand. Holly still struggles with her anxiety sometimes but has the tools to cope and understand it.

SOCIAL ANXIETY: NOTES

Chapter 9
Key Issue Number 7
The Sensory Stuff

What is it?

Ok so this is another big one for our ADHD teens.

These kinds of difficulties are sometimes diagnosed as Sensory Processing Disorder and is a complex condition that I don't claim to know enough about to go into too much detail here. I am aware however that it can be important in career planning and is something to take seriously if your teen is voicing concerns and is practising the avoidance techniques as described below.

If you are regularly experiencing sensory difficulties you may have SPD. In adults, this can show itself in lots of different ways. If you relate to any of these as a parent is may be easier to understand the reactions in your child:

- Over sensitive feelings to light, texture, sound or smells. However, it could also mean that you just don't notice the above.
- Crowded & noisy places make you anxious and overwhelm you.
- Struggling with your balance or co ordination when overloaded with some sensory stimuli.
- Feeling tense and tired when you experience certain environments.
- Avoiding certain social situations as they make you feel overwhelmed.
- Seeking out or avoiding certain sensory experiences.

All these types of symptoms can be quite mild up to really severe. It can be a very complex condition that needs further investigation if you are finding certain situations impossible.

What does it look like in your ADHD teen?

It has a HUGE impact and is often misunderstood as a reluctance to progress or just making excuses not to. Stubbornness, a lack of motivation or laziness.

Sensory processing difficulties can often be a part of ADHD and involves how your teen's brain copes with different smells, noises, sights, textures and the environment. As their parent you have probably noticed some reactions to, for example, particular foods. You probably have put this down to fussy eating and may have tried the old fashioned "sit there until you eat it technique."

It is more likely to be a sensory reaction to the smell, texture & look of the food before they have even tasted it.

So, it goes like this:

You have a fantastic job idea that you think will suit them. You rush into their room and interrupt a key point in their game clutching a vacancy or a career idea, confident in the fact that you have finally cracked it. The answer to all their frustrations and lack of activity. Your excitement is palpable. You hand over your suggestion with a smug grin on your face!

Your teen gives it a cursory glance combined with an eye roll and then throws it back at you with a 'No'.

You can't believe it. How can this be! You probably then act negatively due to the disappointment, frustration and irritation that your wonderful idea has been cast away without some serious consideration and a lovely parent to teen discussion about the pros and cons. You try to reason with them. You try to persuade them otherwise. You still get a resounding 'No' and maybe a 'Just get out!'

One of the reasons that this happens is usually because of ADHDs' common comorbidities. Sensory processing difficulties combined with a dose of anxiety.

As with lots of ADHD traits and symptoms, average senses can be turbo charged. Feelings are magnified and multiplied. Everything can just feel too much. Your teenager is not reacting negatively to annoy you (although your reaction may give them a dopamine hit!) They are trying to communicate that a particular environment would be just too much for them.

What does it look like in career planning?

If you were to consider a position as a chef, you could probably imagine yourself in a reasonably warm environment working to deadline in a practical/creative way. Your ADHD teen with sensory processing difficulties may be able to imagine an area with lights that are too bright. A space that is too loud and crowded with people. An area than is too hot. Lots of intense smells. Throw some deadlines and high expectations in the mix and your teen maybe able to work out that they would be overwhelmed within minutes. By 'overwhelmed' I mean that they are self-aware enough to know that this job would trigger their anxiety, and they would feel uncomfortable in a sensory way. This would make it difficult to focus and complete tasks. In fact, they may get so overloaded with smells, lights, noises etc that they experience sensory overwhelm and either shut down completely or experience a 'melt down'.

You can see that if your teen responds negatively to a job idea but cannot articulate why, you need to accept it as they know what is too much for them. A Careers Adviser may be able to help them explore the reasons in more depth and find alternatives that are not so difficult for them to cope with. Or they may be able to tell you on a different day when things are less emotionally charged. Accept that their self-awareness is a good thing and will save them from ending up in a job that causes them a great deal of stress.

Saying no to everything/Avoidance: In my experience as a Careers Adviser, ADHDers that have sensory concerns can often just say no to a suggested idea without being able to talk about why. It takes a fair amount of skill to get to the bottom of the reasons why it doesn't appeal. They tend to shut down and avoid talking about it as they may feel silly or that you just won't understand. There are lots of emotions involved here as they probably don't really understand why they feel so passionately about something that seems so inconsequential to others.

By saying no to everything, they can avoid environments that will cause sensory overload. If you get this wrong, you will find that the interaction can end here, and they will refuse to get involved in anymore discussions about their future. They will feel foolish and as if they cannot cope with anything. It takes patience, empathy and clever use of open questions to understand what is going on here.

One idea: If your ADHD teen has a job idea that they repeat to anyone and everyone who asks but cannot say why, where the idea came from or what they can imagine themselves doing when engaged in the job - in my experience this can be a deflection technique to avoid talking about jobs/careers in general. I have talked about this with some of the other issues that I have highlighted in this book when career planning with your ADHD teen. I have heard it described as 'throwing him a bone'! For example, if they say 'teaching', the parent/adviser will just talk about that and they will be left alone. The skill is to try and get them to visualise an average day to see how much they actually know about it. It is often very little, and they quickly start to back track when challenged. They begin to look anxious as their plan has been foiled. You can then look at the reasons why the job they had hidden behind is not for them and learn more about the types of things that they would find difficult from a sensory perspective.

Procrastination: I have explored this in an earlier chapter however, the reason for the indecision could possibly be a sensory one! Your ADHD teen may be unable to decide on any type of job or career plan. They will have so many on their possible list and go back and try to weigh up which the best option is. The reason for this may be a sensory one. Attempting to visualise themselves experiencing the job and how it would feel.

How we can help

The way to look at difficulties with sensory processing when career planning is very similar to the techniques used in the last chapter and focus on strengths & weaknesses to work out where the issues lie.

- **Strengths & Weaknesses**: Try and work these out with your teen as described in the last chapter. Just to recap - Keep the 30-minute time limit, keep the humour! Start with the weaknesses and create a middle list, and then a list of strengths. You can move them around putting them on different lists as your discussion evolves. Try and guide rather than tell what to do. Don't disagree or try and correct their feelings. Show them that there will always be aspects of jobs that they will find more difficult than others, but they can work towards or seek help in certain areas. Unlike the issues with self-esteem, you are focussing on sensory issues here. Using open questions, you can ask e.g. "Why do you think that you would feel shy in a work environment?" "How does the thought of working in a big office feel?" "Do you think that you would feel more confident in an outdoor job?" "Can you imagine what it would feel like to work in a restaurant?" etc. You can follow this up with some closed questions such as "Does working outdoors feel more comfortable?"

- **Tools:** once you have been able to talk openly about sensory difficulties with your teen you may find that they are relieved to find out that it can be an ADHD thing. You can begin to look at ways of coping with certain environments. E.g. headphones to cancel out loud noises etc.

- **Occupational Therapy**: it is critical to lean on strengths when it comes to sensory issues that are affecting career planning. Sometimes, we need to let the experts help. Occupational Therapists are skilled in looking at sensory sensitivities that get in the way of pursuing dreams. E.g. if one of our teens was really interested in attending a vocational programme to train to be a mechanic but struggled with bright lights, loud noises and the overwhelming chaos of a busy garage environment, an OT can provide valuable support. They work with our teenagers to identify triggers, develop strategies and make accommodations that make the environment more manageable. They can also help them develop emotional regulation strategies giving them tools to stay calm and focussed in situations where they may feel stressed. Occupational therapy for ADHD is used far more in the U.S. than the U.K. and appears to be really useful. If your teen is really struggling you can request a referral from the NHS but be prepared to look into private support if this is an option for you. Hopefully it will become more available as understanding grows.

SENSORY STUFF: AN EXAMPLE

Charlie

Back story: Charlie was diagnosed with ADHD very early due to struggling with her behaviour and hyperactivity in the classroom. She was prescribed medication at age 7 which enabled her to focus in class and she was then able to achieve academically.

Charlie did well in High School and was able to gain high grades in her GCSEs through a combination of support from school and regular medication which helped with her ADHD symptoms.

Charlie absolutely loved biology and felt that she wanted to go into nursing all the way through her studies. She has managed to do well in her 6th form using the same techniques that worked for her at GCSE as she was in a very familiar environment.

Charlie is the first in her family to stay on into further education and her parents are very proud of her. Her mum is a single parent to 3 children and Charlie is the youngest. Mum has 2 jobs in hospitality and works long hours. Charlie has developed a good routine and is trusted to take her own medication and get herself to 6th form. This has helped her confidence and independence, and she has thrived in this environment. Charlie's older sisters have left home and have families of their own. Her career focus has helped her progression as she feels that she is working towards her passion. Her Dad lives away but plays an active role in her life.

Although Charlie has done a lot of research into nursing, she hasn't had the opportunity to get any work experience until her 6th form placement early in year 13. As she had turned 18 she was able to go to her local hospital to spend some time on a ward.

On Charley's first day there, however, she suffered a panic attack and had to go home. She felt that she couldn't continue with the placement and became absolutely devastated. She was so disappointed that the career that she had been working towards seemed to be unobtainable for her. Her mum was really frustrated with her and couldn't understand what had gone so wrong. Charlie couldn't explain and just got emotional when trying to discuss it.

Charlie came in for careers advice as she felt that she needed to investigate alternative options. She was very emotional and appeared very low as this was a conversation that she didn't want to be having. She could just see her once bright future disappearing and being forced down a route that she wasn't interested in.

How to turn it round

Slow it down. For Charlie, the reality of the job that she had dreamed about was all too much. The option of having a gap year after her A levels to gain some experience had never been suggested. The realisation that this was even an option gave Charlie so much relief and breathing space.

Questions: Charlie was able to identify what feelings she experienced on her placement with the help of careers adviser questioning. It can be helpful to seek professional advice when your teen is struggling to articulate their thoughts and feelings. She was able to talk about her dislike of the bright lights, the smell and the noise of the ward. She felt that this had maybe triggered her anxiety and she became overwhelmed. Charlie had never been in this type of environment before…even as a patient…and so it was a big shock to her. In many ways she had been sheltered by a very supportive school environment without being pushed to go anywhere else.

She was able to realise that her panic attack had been sensory overwhelm and that these were things that she wanted to work on. She was still very keen to pursue her nursing career but needed slow adjustment. She was so relieved that this may be possible and now understood her response to her placement.

Occupational Therapy: Charlie & Mum were unaware that Charlie's issues were something that an occupational therapist could help with. Mum took her to see her GP and she was referred for support on her sensory needs.

Time: Charlie realised that she could spend a year getting some more work experience at her pace. By taking it slowly with the help of an Occupational Therapist she could experience several different environments and adjust to her sensory triggers. One bad experience does not mean that she had to forgo her future dream for good.

RESULT

Charlie took two years out of her studies. She worked with an Occupational Therapist and understood herself and her behaviours better. She got a part time job in a residential care home which she loved. She coped with her sensory overwhelm and became aware of how she could help herself if she became too anxious. However, with time she adjusted to the lights, noise and smell that she had struggled with. She also took some hours working in a bar that her Mum worked in. The emotional support of having her mum there also helped her to adjust to this environment. She felt far more confident that she could cope with lots of different types of places.

Charlie started her Nursing degree last year and is currently in her 2nd year and progressing well.

SENSORY STUFF: NOTES

Chapter 10
Key Issue Number 8
ADHD Freeze
(a.k.a. Overwhelm)

What is it?

The next issue that may well be affecting your teen is the feeling of being overwhelmed. If too much information is presented around a similar time, the ADHD brain can feel completely paralysed and frozen.

One of the body's defence responses is to freeze when under a perceived or real imminent threat. Imagine yourself at age 16 again with teachers mounting up the pressure about your impending exams and revision. At the same time, family maybe asking what it is that you are going to do the following year. Negatively comparing yourself with peers who seem to be so much further ahead. All this is going on when hormonal activity is at a high due to puberty and general adolescent angst. Then throw in some executive functioning issues caused by ADHD that I described earlier... FREEZE! Like a rabbit caught in the head lights! No more information allowed in. The brain is full and for now, closed for business.

This means that no more information will go in and any idea of planning and carrying out tasks will be impossible.

I will say it again! Emotional maturity of your teen with ADHD is probably approximately 3 years behind that of a neurotypical young person. The whole prospect of planning for the future and all it entails is probably terrifying with feelings of 'why I aren't I ready when everyone else is?' That feeling of not being grown up enough. It is no wonder that the brain shuts down and avoids new information that is stressful.

What does it look like in your ADHD teen?

ADHD freeze can appear like your child is avoiding or ignoring what is about to happen. It may look like they don't care and would rather do anything else other than think about the issues that you feel are most important.

In fact, the opposite of this is true. There are just too many thoughts and emotions going on that make it difficult to convey what is really going on in their mind. Too much information so that the brain can just not take in anymore. This then can look like task avoidance and laziness. Doing absolutely nothing. Lack of interest.

Any initial motivation that was in place earlier in the year and that you were so encouraged by has disappeared.

As parents or professionals working with these young people, there needs to be an acceptance that they are probably terrified. It's a huge step when you are not as emotionally mature as your peers.

I think that there is a valid argument in slowing everything down for our teens with ADHD. Although verbally and academically on track, they are probably just not ready for that next step at the same time as neurotypical teenagers. The fact that they are forced into moving forward at a certain time due to school terms etc, causes additional pressure and stress on an immature brain.

Your teen may just go with the flow and copy what everyone else is doing. For example, in the UK, most young people stay on into school sixth forms at 16 to study higher level qualifications. This requires choosing what subjects you would like to pursue further and cutting down your breadth of study to include only 3 to 4 subjects or one vocational area. Your child may just drift along and do this so that it delays making what they perceive as a huge decision that they are just not ready for.

This route is fine if they are academically able and have quite clear ideas, but for many it is just being able to be with friends, attend a safe place that they know and delay the decision as it is stressful. They may follow the same route as a sibling or just do what their parents want them to do. They have blocked that decision out and avoided the issue. It was just too difficult.

So, what you assume is laziness and lack of interest, is in fact ADHD Freeze. They are simply overwhelmed.

What does it look like in career planning?

I have worked with many young people that are struggling with ADHD Freeze, and this is what I have seen:

People Pleaser: this is the young person whose first careers discussion goes well. They engage and have realistic discussions about their next steps and ideas. You agree on a way forward and summarise tasks for them to complete by their next appointment. They are polite, articulate and thank you for your help. As an adviser you feel a sense of job satisfaction having moved a young person on to a bright future.

Then, one of two things happens. Either they turn up for their next appointment looking less motivated and having completed NOTHING on the agreed list of tasks with plenty of excuses OR they just don't turn up at all. So confusing when they appeared engaged and motivated in your initial contact. What went wrong? You start to worry about whether they have had a nasty accident, or something dreadful happened in their life. It just can't be lack of interest as they were so engaged. The truth is that the first appointment was more about pleasing you than them. They went along with it and then immediately blocked it out. Too much too soon. ADHD Freeze.

Rabbit Caught in Headlights: this ADHD teenager looks terrified. Eyes wide and hardly speaks. They appear as if they just want this dreadful interaction over with and to get out as quickly as possible. This is an uncomfortable one-sided conversation for the adviser who tends to cut things short to avoid the intolerable atmosphere! Afterwards the adviser will think that the young person was just not interested and so keep any follow up to a minimum.

What has in fact happened is that they just cannot take on board anymore information as their brain is too full or stressed. ADHD Freeze.

Zombie: This young person appears shut down. They don't really speak and maybe keep a hood up or a coat on as a barrier. They often have a frustrated parent with them who starts to get angry with them due to their perceived lack of interest and that they are coming across as rude. The whole interaction is very difficult as the teen avoids answering questions and responds with one-word answers. They are classed as 'hard to help' and 'disengaged'. Both terms are accurate, but the reason is a combination of being unable to take the information in and an overwhelmed/stressed brain.

Heightened Emotions: This teen is the opposite of the one above in the way that they present. However, the reasons behind their behaviour are the same. They will probably appear quite anxious and on edge. They also may be with a concerned parent who has become worried about their child's mental health and lack of direction. There maybe some engagement in your discussion initially but it will soon result in tears or complete shutdown. The interaction will then need to end quickly. This is difficult to see and is a sign of overwhelm. It is all just too much for the ADHD teenager. Common assumptions are that they are 'spoilt' or 'full of drama'. This isn't the case and is a sign that the way ahead needs to change. This is often seen in undiagnosed ADHD which is unsupported by medication and understanding.

How can we help?

Slow it Down: as I have mentioned previously, the ADHD brain is emotionally immature when compared to their neurotypical peers. This means that the speed of transition from one year to the next is maybe just too fast for them. Don't add to this by expecting career planning to be as fast. Does it matter if they have a 'maturing' year whereby they do some self-reflection and catching up? They can fill it with some voluntary work, part time jobs, hobbies etc that will look great on application forms. There is really no rush. There is less chance the brain will freeze and become overwhelmed if you proceed at a measured pace.

Keep it light: Humour and a light-hearted approach are essential. Most ADHD teens are lucky enough to have excellent senses of humour. Use this to get the best out of their complex brains and reduce the chances of ADHD Freeze. If you become preachy and in teacher-mode, the young person will become more stressed, and the brain will refuse to take anything else in.

Shorten it: Adolescence and ADHD equals short is best! Keep sessions short, snappy and often. The 30-minute rule that I mentioned in an earlier chapter is key. Introduce a new idea or option each time. Cut long explanations to a minimum. Do your best not to overwhelm. Remember that by checking in and asking, "Are you ok to carry on?" the people pleaser will say yes when they mean NO so, take control of the timing of sessions and stick to it.

Bite sized Tasks: Keep any action points that you want completed to a minimum. One at a time. Don't overwhelm or it just won't get done. Be patient and move forward slowly.

Alternative options: There is a decent chance that your ADHDer has zoned out of any careers talk at school and has not taken in what options are available. This will be partly due to fear/stress and partly due to information overload. You will need to introduce each option slowly so that it sinks in with lots of reassurance that they don't have to follow the crowd. You will need to reduce the stress of change and keep in mind that their anxiety will probably be high due to this. Alternative options can be exciting which the ADHD brain loves. For example, would an apprenticeship route suit them better than continued study?

ADHD FREEZE: AN EXAMPLE

Olivia

Back Story: Olivia was described as a bright but 'naughty' child at primary school. She was very chatty and often disruptive in lessons. She often found herself sitting alone so as not to distract others and would race through her work sometimes making careless mistakes.

Due to keeping on top of her learning and coping well with her schoolwork, Olivia was entered into a test for a selective all girl's school in the area at age 11. Although appearing anxious about the test, she passed with a high mark. This meant that she could attend a very academic and prestigious secondary school in her local area.

Olivia started school and settled reasonably well although she missed the friends that she had at primary school who had gone to less academic schools and this caused her some anxiety.

Soon she was expected to hand in homework and complete revision for tests in her new school. Olivia found it impossible to motivate herself and complete this at the end of a school day. She often arrived home exhausted but was unsure why.

Her parents were in well paid jobs and Olivia lived in a very affluent part of the town. Her sister had achieved high grades at GCSE and had gone on to university with no problems. Teachers started to comment that she was wasting her potential and was a lazy student. She found herself slipping behind the other girls in her class. This made her feel even more anxious, but she tried to not show it and put on a mask for school time.

The aspirations that teachers and parents had of Olivia were high and she was expected to attend university like her sister. They could not understand why she wasn't achieving, and she began getting into trouble and receiving detentions. She became withdrawn and emotional, and her school attendance started to suffer.

Olivia was by now surrounded by negative comments and feelings from everyone around her. Friendships had become problematic as she felt that she just didn't fit in at school. She felt that nobody understood her and that she didn't belong anywhere. Home and school had become a battleground.

During her final year, Olivia stopped attending school altogether. She had become so anxious and felt that she could not keep up with her peers. Her parents realised that something wasn't right and started to access some support for her mental health. School work was sent home and Olivia managed to pass her GCSEs with high grades.

It was agreed that the atmosphere of the school was the problem so Olivia was enrolled in a 6th form college to study her A levels. Everyone agreed that this was a brilliant fresh start for her and would be the answer to the issues that she had come across in school. A couple of her friends had also enrolled, and Olivia was keen to embrace her new life.

In a matter of weeks, the same pattern started to emerge. Olivia was struggling to concentrate in her new 90-minute lectures and was failing to hand in homework. Teachers again began to judge her harshly and make her stay behind to try and finish incomplete work. Although she now had more support with her mental health, Olivia once again started to feel that she didn't fit in and stopped attending college.

Olivia's parents were again frustrated with her and didn't understand why she just couldn't do her work.

How to turn it round

Acceptance: that Olivia was overwhelmed and struggling. Advice from GP re what could be causing her poor mental health. ADHD assessment & diagnosis.

ADHD diagnosis & medication: helped Olivia to focus on what she needed to do next and helped her anxiety.

Slow it down: Suggestion that Olivia take a year out to reassess her likes & dislikes. Recover from her negative experiences and gain some positive new ones.

Work experience: Complete some work experience and gain a part time job. Olivia started working in a café which she loved.

Voluntary work: Olivia also started some voluntary work with animals.

Careers research & alternative options: Manageable time spent researching alternative options that would suit her learning style more.

Reassurance: that her undiagnosed ADHD massively impacted her school years and was the reason that she had felt unhappy for so long.

RESULT

Olivia really enjoyed her year out and felt that she had lots of new skills to put on application forms. She learnt how to manage her ADHD and used her medication when she needed to focus.

She realised that she didn't want to attend university and that she would prefer an apprenticeship route. She was successful in gaining an apprenticeship with a local charity supporting people with disabilities. She really enjoyed this and made lots of new friends of all ages. She was now looking into the future positively.

ADHD FREEZE: NOTES

Chapter 11
Key Issue Number 9
Time Blindness

What is it?

Time blindness is probably the most overlooked cognitive symptom of ADHD.

Research suggests that people with ADHD struggle with estimating time. They can also struggle with an overwhelming feeling that time is passing too quickly and that they haven't completed tasks that they need to have finished. Almost as if their 'internal clock' is just a little faulty.

The ability to estimate how much time you need or how much time has passed is just a bit off! The wiring of the brain with ADHD makes it more difficult to judge time. The upshot of this can be poor mental health as the constant inability to do things on time can cause panic and anxiety. Time blindness can also impact relationships – both personally and professionally. So, yes, it can be a tricky one!

There are types of time blindness that it is important to spot as being the key issue that causes the struggles.

Estimating time: the ability to estimate how much time has passed. Working out how much time is needed to complete a task.

Managing time: the ability to plan & manage time. Working this out requires planning skills, concentration, memory and co-ordination.

Time anticipation: how quickly is a task approaching & when to start acting on it.

Time sequencing: sequencing tasks or events in the correct order that they have occurred.

Time reproduction: the ability to repeat the same task again for the same amount of time it took previously.

What does it look like in your ADHD teen?

Time blindness as a symptom of ADHD is probably overlooked in young children. Let's face it, we are more likely to complete tasks for them, get them ready and out of the door, drive them to places etc. This has probably caused some level of stress for parents but at least your child was able to complete the things that they set out to do without ruining relationships or opportunities.

So, you knew getting them ready for things was annoying…but what you didn't realise was that this was part of their ADHD. When you get into the teenage years, you expect to be able to take a step back in this way. But no!

It's important to stress here that not all individuals with ADHD struggle with time blindness. And for those that do, there are types of time blindness that may impact most. So, your first job is to work out if it is an issue and if it is, what are the things that they really struggle with.

Your teen may be very last minute with deadlines. You will know this by the rushed homework assignments and late-night revision. Alongside this comes the tension and stress that feeling unprepared gives them.

You may have a familiar picture of your child speeding down the road to catch a bus or meet a friend with only seconds to spare. Or sometimes being so late and unprepared that they don't bother going at all.

You may have to deal with the fallout from problematic relationships with friends/partners that they have let down through not being on time or completing something that they said they would. Good luck with that one!

Your teenager may over promise having no perception of the limits of their time and productivity.

'Yeah, I can write a script for that part of the school play…'

OR

'Yeah of course I can come to your house before I go to college'

You know that they will find it impossible, but they won't agree!

Your teen may be known as 'the late one'. Chronic lateness for absolutely everything. Or the reverse of that, the inability to judge time - so being ready far too early. Sitting outside buildings before they open.

Hanging round outside friend's houses. Walking the streets before job interviews. People assume that this is your child being really organised – it isn't. It is ADHD time blindness!

You may recognise the emotional impact of time blindness on your teen. The awful self-disappointment when things have gone wrong again, and they don't really understand why. The guilt when they have been late for something that was actually hugely important to them, and they have let someone they care about down.

What does it look like in career planning?

From the above descriptions, it is easy to see how problematic time blindness can be during transition periods such as career decisions for ADHD teenagers. It is simple to see how they get left behind when compared with their neuro typical peers.

From my experience, this is what time blindness can look like in ADHD young people in careers interviews:

- **Stuck in 'waiting mode'** i.e. waiting in limbo for a job or college interview a long time before it happens. This time is usually unproductive, and they literally just wait for that thing to happen. The interview feels so much closer than it actually is and means that they just can't apply for other things while they are waiting. It appears that they have tunnel vision and are unable to explore other options available. This can be so frustrating for parents when you are desperate for them to keep their options open.

- **Panicky**: ADHDers appear concerned that they have lost track of time, and they are panicking about the future. They make impulsive decisions only to then talk themselves out of it. They will bounce from one idea to another. They can feel that they are losing grip of time when the reality is that they have plenty to be able to research and decide thoroughly.

- **Overestimating the time available:** This teen looks very relaxed and is usually brought to the careers appointment by a fraught looking parent. They don't understand the rush and think that they have all the time in the world to decide what they want to do.

- **Unable to estimate:** An ADHDer that is describing work experience or out of school activities will be unable to estimate the time spent doing it. They just find it impossible and will massively under or overestimate. Not great when trying to construct a winning CV!

- **Hyperfocus:** Some young people have just lost total track of time by hyper focussing on an interest and have missed deadlines for applications etc. For example, the teen that has spent every waking moment playing a particular computer game only to find that they have missed everything, and their friends have moved on! The teen that volunteered in an animal shelter and cared passionately about rescue animals missed out on considering what they wanted to do long term as they didn't have the brain space. The current hyperfocus takes over everything.

- **Estimating how long ago:** When concentrating on their past experiences, some young people can find it impossible to estimate how long ago something happened. E.g. how long ago did you leave school? They are just unable to tell you. They look at parents for some idea of how long ago key parts of their lives actually occurred.

- **Living in the present:** Some ADHD teens only have the ability to look at ideas for the present and the very short term. This is difficult when qualifications chosen need to link in with a long term aim for example. Or when you consider suggesting they do a certain job as a stepping stone into something else. They struggle with looking to the future and find it impossible to imagine themselves in 10 years' time. The here and now is everything.

- **Deadline date difficulties:** As part of most career planning sessions, the young person will agree and leave with some action points to carry out. They will usually have dates that the actions need to be done by put next to them. ADHD youngsters affected by time blindness may find it challenging to put this together in the first place and then impossible to follow it. This is impacted by their struggles with organisation too.

- **Procrastination:** ADHD teens that I have seen with no plans and have left it all to the last minute tend to be procrastinators as discussed in the previous chapter. They have put off tasks to do with their future due to over thinking them which results in them not being done at all.

How Can We Help?

Acceptance: The first and essential part of helping with the issue of time blindness is accepting it exists as a problem for your child. Accepting that it is a massive part of their ADHD and how their brain is wired. Yes, it can be hugely irritating when your teen is late for almost everything, but it does not mean that they are lazy or unconcerned about what they are trying to do. Disciplining it out of them will not help. You will only succeed in damaging your relationship and creating an unpleasant and sometimes toxic atmosphere at home.

As mentioned earlier, ADHD young people are so used to being told off. Told that they are not good enough. Compared to others who seem to do things so effortlessly. Imagine the impact on their mental health when they just hear negative things about themselves. Accept that time blindness is part of their disability and then you can look at ways to help.

Time Blindness Type: In the sections above I described types of time blindness. Try your best to work out which type is your ADHDer's particular flavour! It may be that they are affected by all of them, or are a couple of them more prevalent?

For example, it could be that your teen is unable to **estimate time** as accurately as others, so they have a compulsion to be ridiculously early for everything. This can be as frustrating to others as those that are late for everything. 'Why is he ready to go out so early & not doing anything else?' 'Why is she hanging round outside when it's not time to go inside?!'

Or the young person who struggles with **time anticipation**. Seemingly unaware how quickly a task is approaching & when to start acting on it. "Why haven't you applied for the job I gave you? You've missed the deadline now!"

Once you have worked out what is going on for your child, the next step is to find some ways to help support them.

So, we've accepted that time blindness is an issue for our ADHDer and worked out which particular part of this they struggle with...if not all. We now need to put things in place to help that will ensure that timing isn't an issue and therefore reduce the stress and anxiety surrounding it.

SMART PHONES:

Use Calendars: By this I don't mean the one you have hanging up in the kitchen that has photos of cute puppies on...unless this really interests your child of course. Technology can be a curse for teenagers, but it can also be an absolute godsend. Most young people are now lucky enough to own a smart phone and, in some cases, a smart watch too. Both these devices include calendars. Key deadlines or events can be set into the calendar that sound an alarm. Wonderful! You can even set a series of alarms that give a warning to start preparing for something. Be careful not to give too much of a time buffer though as your teenager will forget the alarm has happened and get drawn into whatever they were doing before! Your ADHDer will then need to learn to take notice of and trust the alarms and reminders set. This may take practice, but they will help enormously. Specific ADHD timer apps can now also be purchased. Check these out if you wish but in my experience the reminders & timers already on your phone work just as well.

App Blockers: App blockers are settings on your phone that can restrict access at specific times or can put time limits on. If your phone is linked to theirs, you can do this from your own device. If not, you will need to gain access to your child's device to put the settings on. Instructions on how to do this are readily available online or check in with a tech savvy friend so that you are clued up before mentioning it. Be prepared for some push back and attitude to this from your teen. As the majority live in the here and now, they won't understand the need for this. Be ready with examples of when things have been difficult for them timewise and discuss it calmly with them. Try not to make them feel shame or guilt about struggling with time blindness. Stress that it is an aid to help with their ADHD. You may need to introduce the idea first and build up to it. Get another trusted adult (preferably with ADHD themselves) on board to explain why it's important and reassure them that they will still have access to their beloved device. This will be easier if the luxury of having their own phone has come with boundaries agreed at the start…. if not, be brave. They will hopefully understand the benefit eventually and maybe even thank you!

Control ADHD hyperfocus: there is likely to be something in your teenager's life that is hugely important to them. Something that they literally hyperfocus on. Hyperfocus is a very common symptom of ADHD, and you can read up more about the impact online if you wish. For the purposes of the topic of this book, it is enough to be aware that an ADHD hyperfocus can be all encompassing. A very common example of this can be computer games. Lots of parents will struggle to understand how their distracted child can focus for hours on something like computer games. The focus is so intense that they will not notice the passage of time i.e. time blindness. Research suggests that this is due to the low dopamine levels associated with ADHD so that anything that they really want to do introduces the feeling of reward when focussed on. The advantages of this is enormous productivity when completing something that they love and this is often used in jobs really successfully. The negative side can be the hours that pass without your young person even knowing what time it is. They can be so absorbed that everything else is blocked out. They won't hear your shouts of 'dinner's ready!' or 'you need to do your college application'.

We can successfully use smart devices again here. Hyperfocus needs to be discussed with your ADHDer so that they know why they do this. Then you can both decide how to control it. A series of alarms may need to be used to break into a very focussed ADHD brain. Talk to your child as they will know best what breaks in and what doesn't. It is unlikely to be your increasingly frustrated voice!

The strategies we are looking at here will all involve your teenager's ability to understand their condition and have recognised that they need some help with managing it. Not an easy step to get to but you will get there. Take all these steps in a calm manner and have patience.

TRACKING TIME:

Visual tracking of time can be a useful aid for time blindness. This can be a very individual thing so your child can try a few to see what works for them. Examples of these are:

Multiple Wall Clocks: Having a clock that is visible in each room can be very beneficial to ADHD time blindness. So, wherever you go in the house you can check the time. Outside, always having a watch on that you can check the time can be essential. Basic but highly effective. The downside is remembering to check the time of course!

Timers: as discussed earlier, timers can be a great idea. A timer that goes off every 30 minutes and literally gives you a time check can help to structure your day. This can also be done on a watch and could just be a vibration rather than a sound so that you don't disrupt others. You can set different tones or vibrations for hourly reminders and half hourly so you can keep track of where you are in that particular activity. E.g. during a job interview you could set a smart watch to vibrate when you are half an hour through it.

Music: listening to music can be a great way for your teen to track time. Most tracks are about 5 minutes long so allowing yourself 6 tracks to complete a piece of homework can work wonders to focus the brain and be aware of where you are up to. Another 4 tracks to have a shower etc. This can be a more entertaining version of time tracking for your child. They could use the same playlist when getting ready for a particular event. E.g. getting ready for 'college play list' finishing with a track that means "Leave the House Now!"

Phone timer: setting a visual countdown on a smart phone can help focus the brain. E.g. Set the time for 60 mins to complete an application form and your teenager will be able to see the time ticking away. You find that the majority of the form is completed in the last few minutes, but it is done.

TIME MANAGEMENT TECHNIQUES:

There are loads of books written on time management. Ironically, most people struggling with time blindness would find reading such a book almost impossible! Here is a very quick summary about what such books usually contain. If you think one of the techniques may work with your child and help them with career planning (and other things) feel free to research in more depth:

Breaking Big Goals Down: this is about breaking an end goal down into small, achievable chunks. This is useful in ADHD as it takes the stress and anxiety out of being unable to know how to move forward. It also shows progress clearly so that your child will be able to track how far along they are in completing their goal. This could be used when considering a career idea that needs significant work to be able to achieve. For example, your teen is interested in Law, so the first step is to research it as a career area. Once that is achieved, they can move on to making sure that they achieve the relevant qualifications etc. Books looking at this as a time management technique tend to have charts and journals to complete that break tasks down. Useful if you think your child would use them or if you can complete it with them.

Time blocking: time management books can also talk about the time blocking technique. This is about dividing time into multiple blocks visually. Each block is dedicated to one single task or a group of similar tasks. Again, this can prove useful but does need significant motivation to complete.

Pomodoro Technique: this is a well-documented technique that involves 25-minute blocks of time followed by a 5-minute break. It can be adjusted depending on what works for your child and what task is being attempted. There are many smart phone apps that help with this technique as well as many books. Have a look and see what you think by a quick search online.

So, there we are. Time blindness and the challenges it brings your ADHD teenager. The good news is that this one gets easier with maturity and techniques that help become recognised and used as part of a person's day to day routine. Research also suggests that ADHD medication works well in improving time perception and management.

TIME BLINDNESS: AN EXAMPLE

Ellie

Back Story: Ellie was diagnosed with Combined ADHD in her final year of secondary school. Her Mum fought hard for her to be assessed and diagnosed as she was described as lively, chatty and anxious throughout school. Often getting into trouble for her behaviour and not completing her classwork or homework. Not studying towards her exams and being late for lessons and school in general. Mum received lots of criticism regarding her parenting style that was 'perceived' to be to blame for Ellie's chronic lateness. Ellie received no support from school to assist her with her time blindness as the diagnosis came too late to have any impact. Mum & Ellie struggled on alone with Mum trying to get Ellie to see that she needed to adhere to a timetable during the day. This often led to arguments between them and affected both their mental health.

Ellie had a large group of friends at school who seemed to be very like her but nobody whom she could rely on. She often found herself in isolation and in detentions for not conforming to deadlines and targets.

Ellie went on to obtain a few GCSEs and teachers agreed that she had underachieved. This upset her as she knew that she had tried to work hard but could never seem to get things done on time.

Ellie left school without making any plans for the future. She thought that she had loads of time and was just relieved to be out of an environment that she didn't like. Mum tried to get her to apply to college, but Ellie could never get down to doing it and missed the deadline. This caused more arguments between her and her Mum. She was now socially isolated as she did not have the routine of school to rely on for friendships. She began to suffer from anxiety and panic attacks.

Ellie had some ideas about becoming a Paramedic as she really enjoyed being there for people. She also thought it would be exciting and varied and she knew that she was calm in a crisis. She had no idea how she could make this happen and couldn't make the time to even find out. When she did stop to think about it for a moment, she was flooded with memories of her failing at school and opinions people seemed to have of her. It was easier to concentrate on watching TV and being on her phone. She has even given up playing for her local football team which she used to love.

Mum was becoming increasingly worried but also frustrated with Ellie. As a single parent she now had no income to support her. She just couldn't understand why Ellie had retreated into herself and wouldn't do anything at all. Mum knew how bright Ellie was and would have loved her to go to college. Mum didn't realise that time blindness was part of her ADHD diagnosis and thought that it just made it difficult for her to concentrate and made her a bit loud and chatty.

The arguments between Ellie and Mum meant the Ellie began spending time at her Nan's house in a different area as life was just too stressful at home.

How to turn it round

Slow it down: the transition needed to be slowed down and the pressure to be taken off both Ellie and Mum. Ellie's emotional maturity needed to develop. Again, taking a gap year was key but making sure it was filled with useful experiences.

Practical support: Ellie needed support with her time blindness, prioritising her ideas and deciding what is important to her.

Accommodation: Ellie's Mum made an appointment for her to come to the Careers Centre. This was an impossible ask for Ellie as she would have been unable to leave the house and get there on time so initial appointments were held at her Nan's house.

Reminders: Reminders of appointment times were sent to her at regular intervals, so she knew to expect a visit. Regular checking in messages were also sent.

Routine: A routine of weekly appointments was established by text which led Ellie to be able to come into the centre rather than be visited. The routine helped her know where she had to be and when.

Smart Phone: Ellie was supported to access calendars and reminders on her phone. She was able to set deadlines for college applications with alarms and reminders that also involved preparation time built in. She started to trust and use this technique as she could see it working. This massively increased her confidence.

Techniques for time management: Ellie was supported to use time management aids such as the Pomodoro technique which helped her to complete her research and applications in small chunks with a break. She was able to send her college application in on time and attend an interview.

RESULT

Ellie was able to start driving lessons which took a lot of her focus during her gap year.

She was able to move back in with her Mum and their relationship improved.

Ellie was offered a place at college to study Health related subjects in line with her long-term aim as a Paramedic which she could now see as a realistic possibility. She began ADHD medication which combined with her time management strategies really helped her to organise her time.

This in turn reduced her anxiety and she felt her time blindness was under control. She felt confident enough to ask for help with timing when she needed it and was able to articulate what and why she had some difficulties with it.

TIME BLINDNESS: NOTES

So, to conclude…

The reason for writing this book is to support parents to help their young people. Professional services are under resourced or still 'don't get it'. In an ideal world, our unique teenagers would be supported by neurodivergence specialists in education and through transition times. We know that currently this is not happening and leaves our children out in the cold. For this reason, I wanted to help equip parents to understand more so that they can fill the gap for their teenagers where possible.

I want to thank you for getting this far. If ADHD is in your genetic make-up, I know that it's no mean feat to reach the conclusion of any book. I have a pile of books by my bed that proves this.

I want to also thank you for caring and wanting to understand more about the young person you have had in mind when you started to read this. Having you by their side will mean their challenges will be less. Whether you are a parent, relative or keyworker…believe me, having a trusted adult to lean on who is willing to learn is EVERYTHING. They will thank you…eventually!

I could have written a much longer book as there are many more traits of ADHD that you may identify as being problematic. However, I have tried to summarise what I see are the main barriers for our young people when facing transition points in their life.

They are in no particular order in their importance. They all matter and have to be navigated in some way by most ADHD teens.

Those that made my short list are **social anxiety, overwhelm, time blindness, procrastination, self-esteem, sensory problems, boredom, masking** and finally, **rejection sensitivity.**

I realise that a book focussing on the difficulties of ADHD can be pretty depressing, however, knowledge is so important when facing challenges. I hope I have been able to show that there are ways to overcome your teenager's struggles.

They so often get overlooked and dismissed as young people who won't achieve much when in fact the opposite is true. It is unfortunately the case that ADHD young people (both diagnosed & undiagnosed) make up a large proportion of the youth unemployment statistics.

They are more vulnerable to slips and trips along the way that I hope this book has explained. They are wrestling with issues that don't impact those described as 'neurotypical' young people in the same way. I have explained a few but there are many more.

Our ADHDers are having to cope with an education and employment system that simply is not set up for their brain type. It means that the obstacles are bigger, and this can have an impact on self-worth and progression along the way.

By reducing the pressure at key transition points and accepting that some young people need to slow the pace and take longer to achieve their dreams, our teenagers will thrive . This should be done without the stigma that can often contribute to poor mental health. Providing nurturing environments that can build confidence and an acceptance of differences in learning style is key to their success. ADHD young people can then show their brilliance and be allowed to bloom and flourish.

They are among the most intelligent, creative, talented and successful people in society. Our teenagers are amazing and with a little support when needed, will progress into the most wonderful, happy & content adults with bright futures.

EXTRAS

1. RESEARCH PILOT DETAILS

2. CAREERS TOOL KIT

3. USEFUL LINKS

4. ADDITIONAL READING

1. RESEARCH PILOT WITH UNEMPLOYED TEENAGERS

As my current role as a Careers Adviser working with unemployed young people, I started to identify ADHD traits in high numbers of them. Their struggles seemed to add up to the same thing. I was constantly identifying anxiety; low self-esteem; problems with focus; poor school attendance; addiction; motivation struggles; etc, etc. I felt strongly that their problems with progression were mainly due to ADHD. Mostly unsupported, misunderstood ADHD!

I was in the perfect position to prove this as this was my job. Providing careers guidance to NEET (not in education, employment or training) young people. So, I set about seeing a sample of 100 young people between the ages of 16 and 25 who were currently unemployed and would be seen by my organisation anyway. The only difference was that I was making a note of those already diagnosed ADHD - and those that weren't were offered the opportunity to take part in a voluntary screening exercise that would identify ADHD traits & symptoms. 98% of young people were happy to be involved in my research and were genuinely interested in what they could find out about themselves.

The results were astonishing. The research found a high prevalence of ADHD traits, both diagnosed and undiagnosed among young people who were NEET and using careers guidance services.

- Almost half of the young people in the pilot (46/100) had a previous ADHD diagnosis.
- Of the remainder, 23/52 (44%) screened as being 'highly likely' to have an ADHD condition.
- 9/52 (36.6%) screened as ADHD being a 'possible' condition.
- Only 10 (19%) screened as ADHD as being 'unlikely'.

So, of the 100 young people that took part, 88 were found to either have an existing ADHD diagnosis or were identified by the screening tool as ADHD being highly likely or possible. Thought provoking and important results.

2. CAREERS TOOL KIT

- **DECISION MAKING: THE TRAINERS ANALOGY!**

A useful analogy I have used with ADHD young people is that of going out shopping to buy a pair of trainers. By firstly talking about the steps we go through when choosing a new piece of footwear (that the vast majority of teens love…but if not, replace 'trainers' with any other item of interest) the idea is that they see making career decisions is not much different! It hopefully takes the fear and pressure away slightly.

We talk about the ideas and worries we may have before we go shopping. So:

- will I feel confident enough to go on my own or will I need someone with me?
- how will I get to the shops?
- where should I keep my money to make sure it's safe?
- have I done enough research on the types of brands I like?
- have I got enough money for the trainers I like?
- what should I do if I feel uncomfortable or need to come home quickly?
- which shops shall I visit?

You can then move on to actually being in the shop.

- Do the trainers look as nice now I can physically see them & touch them?
- Do they have my size in stock?
- Do I need to try a different shop that has more choice or a better price?
- Do you try them on?
- How do they fit?
- Do they look & feel as good as you thought they would?

- Do you need a different size?
- Whom do you ask for advice if you feel unsure?

Then move on to taking the pair of trainers to the till to pay for them.

- have you got enough money with you or in your account?
- what do you do when you are offered a more expensive pair instead?
- what do you do when you are offered insoles, cleaning products, extras to buy at the till?

You can then move on to discussing how you felt after making your purchase.

- Are you happy with your choice?
- Whom do you check with to reassure yourself that you made the right decision?
- What do you do if you feel that you have made the wrong decision?

CONTRACT

What shall we talk about? Let your teenager decide what to talk about and write it down. Tick off each one as you go so you can start again at another time.

Ideas:

School subjects (likes & dislikes, reasons why…)

Outside Interests (likes & dislikes, reasons why…)

Strengths & Weaknesses (what am I good at; what am I not so good at….)

Short Term Ideas/Options After School

(go through each option, likes & dislikes, reasons why…)

For example: school 6th form; college; training; apprenticeship, job, voluntary work

Long Term Ideas

(Reasons why they interest; advantages & disadvantages of job type; what else do I need to find out about it)

ACTION PLAN

Keep it simple. Use bullet points.

Where are you now?

What are you doing in school? What year are you in? What interests do you have?

Aims & Ideas

Any career ideas

Things to Do Next

2 or 3 things to do before the next time!

3. USEFUL LINKS

https://adhduk.co.uk/

https://www.headstuffadhdtherapy.co.uk/

https://www.mind.org.uk/

https://www.additudemag.com/

https://www.verywellmind.com/

https://www.healthline.com/

https://www.youngminds.org.uk/

https://psychcentral.com/

https://www.unlockingadhd.com/

https://www.adhdcentre.co.uk/

https://totallyadd.com/

https://www.nhs.uk/mental-health/children-and-young-adults/mental-health-support/

ADHD PODCASTS:

Parenting ADHD

with Penny Williams

I'm ADHD No You're Not

with Dr Mine Conkbayir & Paul Whitehouse

ADHD Chatter

with Alex Partridge

The ADHD Women's Wellbeing Podcast

with Kate Moryoussef

4. ADDITIONAL READING

How Not to Damage Your ADHD Adolescent

Sarah Templeton 2024

Teachers! How Not to Kill the Spirit in Your ADHD Kids

Sarah Templeton 2022

Career Coaching Your Kids

Montross, Kane & Ginn Jr 2004

Now It All Makes Sense

Alex Partridge 2024

Taking Charge of ADHD: The Complete, Authoritative Guide for Parents

Russell A. Barkley, PhD

Understanding ADHD: A Parents Guide to ADHD in Children

Dr Christopher Green & Dr Kit Chee

Looking After Your Mental Health

Alice James & Louis Stowell 2018

Creative Career Coaching: Theory Into Practice

Hambly L & Bomford C 2018

About the Author

Jenny Booth is an experienced Careers Advisor with a particular interest in neurodiversity and inclusivity. She has carried out research projects to look at the link between ADHD and youth unemployment. Born in Wrexham and now living in Wirral with her husband and son. She enjoys long dog walks and cosy pubs.

www.ingramcontent.com/pod-product-compliance
Ingram Content Group UK Ltd.
Pitfield, Milton Keynes, MK11 3LW, UK
UKHW022240230426
12048UKWH00018BA/1364